HEALING
IN MIND

David Hoffmeister

Healing In Mind
By David Hoffmeister

ISBN: 978-0-9767485-5-7

Copyright © 2000, 2008, 2009 Foundation for the Awakening Mind

Foundation for the Awakening Mind
4443 Station Avenue, rear bldg
Cincinnati, OH 45232, USA

+1 513.898.1364
www.awakening-mind.org
www.course-in-miracles.com

First edition 2008 Joyfully produced by The Messengers of Peace

Printed in the United States of America

Second Printed Edition 2009
Project Healing Press
St. Louis, MO

Foundation for the Awakening Mind

Written by: David Hoffmeister
Compiled by: Ben Gilberti
Edited by: Kirsten Buxton
                Sarah Pilkington
                Jenny Fagerstedt
                Pam Bahr
Cover Art: Sarah Pilkington
Book Design: Sue Sylvia

HEALING IN MIND

David Hoffmeister

EXPRESSIONS OF GRATITUDE

The original version of this book was prepared
with the loving care and attention of Ben Gilberti.
I am grateful to Ben, the Messengers of Peace,
and other contributing volunteers
for their passion in making this material available
in book form so that many can benefit
from the sharing of this Inner Wisdom.

This book, like every aspect of the
non-profit Foundation for the Awakening Mind,
is the fruit of a collaborative effort
of willing and inspired volunteers.
I offer my love and appreciation to the Holy Spirit
and to everyone who asked such sincere questions
and shared their intimate thoughts and feelings
with great trust and deep passion.

I am forever grateful.

Love & Blessings,
David

CONTENTS

Chapter 4

Chapter 5

Biography

References

A Course In Miracles
Reference Abbreviations

T: Text
W: Workbook for Students
M: Manual for Teachers
P: Psychotherapy: Purpose, Process and Practice

Chapter 1

RELEASING ABUSE

Hello David,

Thank you for taking the time to read my message. This may sound sarcastic; however it IS a genuine question. I ask this as a person who was abused, sexually and otherwise, by mostly male family members, virtually from birth. What does it mean by "the script"? Am I supposed to have chosen all this???!!! Is there no punishment for the perpetrators???!!! "Worldly justice" is not possible. I have repressed memory for the most part, and I guess I am still afraid. I feel like, somewhere within I may know the answer, so why am I not "getting it"?! Gggrrrr! (Can you tell? LOL!) If I could let go of all this, how would that prevent these people from continuing to abuse me, even if not physically? One of my abusers is extremely arrogant and believes he has done no wrong. I cannot believe that any Higher Power would agree with that! Are these people simply allowed to carry on with their behavior???!!! Truly, I am not meaning to be sarcastic, or difficult. I am genuinely questioning! Yes... I'm confused!

I tried to live by the Course for years, before I had ever read it. I knew it instinctively, however I also had mental illness, which I did not realize the origins of, until I was around 20 years old. I experience many miracles in the material sense all the time. I also understand the shift in consciousness, though it took an incredible amount of spiritual work on my part and did not prevent things from going wrong in my life from that point on. What am I doing wrong???!!! Sexual abuse "counselors" would say I am doing nothing wrong, but I would truly value your opinion.

Thanks again for your time.

Hello Beloved One,

Thanks for pouring your heart out so openly. Awakening is the simple recognition that Love is Present and only Love exists. Forgiveness is the release of the belief in attack by recognizing that there are not different forms of one lie called ego. Spirit cannot attack or be attacked, and Christ Self is Spirit. There is no injustice to Spirit. All things work together for good. There are no exceptions, except in the ego's judgment. Forgiveness shows that there is no ego Now, for only a reflection of Love remains. The ego was the seeming belief that it is possible to be unfairly treated. I rejoice that God's Will is Love and that Love is real. You are the Christ, forever Perfect. Nothing at all has gone "wrong" in our Reality. You are forever Innocent and I See You. For this Fact I give thanks. I love You forever and ever!!!

Love always, David

ACIM Lesson 157

Hello David,

Lesson 157 states that it brings us to the door where all learning ceases and we catch a glimpse of what lies past the highest reaches it can possibly attain. It ushers in a new experience; a different kind of feeling and awareness. Today you learn to feel the joy of life. But I have had no such experience. Does this mean I am not doing the lessons properly? I have all along very diligently practiced exactly as specified. Now I am beginning to feel dejected and hopeless. What happens to those of us who, even after going through the text and workbook lessons, cannot get salvation? Do we have to die and come back in another life to continue our journey?

I have another question. Even though I am practicing the lessons exceedingly well, there are days when I am unable to proceed to the next lesson. Thus there are days I go without practicing. However after I become less agitated, I restart my practice. Is this alright? However much I try, I cannot practice one lesson per day. Should we strictly follow one lesson a day suggestion for them to be effective?

Thank you for all your help.

Beloved One,

Thanks for writing and for your devotion to Awakening. Think of these Workbook lessons as a laboratory for applying the ideas and putting them into practice. It is wonderful that you are willing to do the lessons. Cultivate and nurture this willingness, and when the feelings of agitation, dejection, or hopelessness arise just apply the lesson of the day to whatever is in your awareness. You were instructed to not do more than one lesson a day, and this does not mean that you cannot stay with a lesson for more than a day if it feels helpful. When you

notice that you are not feeling at peace or judge that you are not experiencing the meaning of what the lesson is pointing to, simply return to the idea of the day.

The lessons are collections of words designed to help train the mind to a new perception of everything and everyone. If you read through the web site at www.awakening-mind.net, you will find many resources that help you deepen into the mind. With devotion and practice these Awakening ideas will feel more and more natural. All the support of the Holy Spirit and the angels is with you in this Awakening. The people you meet and the symbols that reach your awareness will increasingly reflect the deepest desire of your heart: to Awaken in God's Love.

Be not concerned about the seeming "death" of the body. The body is merely a device, a symbol among symbols, used by the Holy Spirit to help Awaken the mind which seems to sleep. Your work with ACIM will help you release the ego's use of the body and world, for the ego's purpose was a death wish. Once this death wish is exposed it is no longer attractive, and it is laid aside forever. Practice the lessons with passion and devotion for the mind is thus made ready to accept complete forgiveness and experience the Truth of Being.

There is an archive and search tool on the Awakening In Christ Yahoo Group web site that can be very helpful. As questions arise about your work with the Workbook or about other topics, this search tool can help in coming to the experience of Clarity. I am joined with you in this holy Purpose, and nothing can prevail against our joining. I am with you all the way Beloved Child of God. Blessings abound! All Glory to God!

Love always, David

An Experiment In Forgiveness

David,

I'm writing to ask for your feedback on my dance with the illusion of good-bad mother. This seems to be my learning edge issue right now, which really came to the forefront when you were here. I appreciate the synchronicity in my 22 year old daughter coming to live with us next week for six weeks while she finishes her studies for her B.A. and saves some money to move into an apartment with a friend. This is my opportunity to face my guilt/fear on a daily basis and bring to the light some deeply held beliefs for release.

Some of my thoughts: She's too loud (she sings beautifully but loud and sometimes when people are sleeping), she's messy (takes a shower in my bathroom and leaves a trail of clothing), she needs money (and I want to give it to her, but then when we can't pay our credit card that month, I feel stupid) and she's careless with money (buying clothes when she can't pay her cell phone) which has led to me paying it and feeling stupid again.

I recognize that these are projections of my fear of bothering people, of not being independent, of needing things from other people, etc., and I could use some words of wisdom from you.

Thanks and see you this summer!

Beloved One,

Thanks for your e-mail. Yes, you are getting a close look at the beliefs and trains of thought you still hold dear and must release. You are much more than a "mother" (good or bad) and during the next six weeks your mind will be shown that this is so. Your responsibility now is to be peaceful and to extend peace. You have a six week experiment of unlearning at hand, and this can offer you great insight and release. Think

of and treat your daughter and yourself as if you have no memory of a past together, as if you are hosting for six weeks a beloved house guest that you adore and respect. Offer only what you experience in your heart as Joyful. Offer only what has no bargains or strings attached.

Do not think and act as though you must please your guest – rather, just feel the Truth that no demands are placed on you except by your own decisions. Imagine that Jesus is staying at your house for six weeks and asks only that you relax and be happy and peaceful. Jesus is not asking you for money, not asking you to pick up after him, and is not asking you to mind anyone's mind except your own. The form that the next six weeks will take is not yours to control, yet moment by moment you must take full responsibility for your own state of mind. You will be "taking the stranger in" and seeing that you cannot be the "keeper" of anyone "else" for there literally is no one "else" to care for. Watching your mind is your full time "job," so to speak, and judging is not a part of your miracle worker "job description."

Whatever you seem to reject you have already judged against. If you perceive a behavior or trait that you dislike you are attempting to project the thought to the world as if it is not in your mind. Yet ideas leave not their source, and you must recognize that you always judge yourself when you judge anybody. Judgment is not an ability that God gave to our Holy Mind. The mother and daughter roles were assigned by the ego, and it matters not if positive or negative attributes were added to the roles. Christ is what you really want to see Now, yet it will seem impossible to see with this Vision until you realize that Love makes no demands.

If peace is your only goal Now, you will think and feel and perceive from the Divine Integrity of the Love within. You will Flow easily. You will neither make demands nor accept demands that seem to be placed on you.

Every moment is a clean, clear, fresh beginning, untarnished by the past – it is a new opportunity to consciously choose what you REALLY want. Every morning when you wake and rise, remember what your goal is. Remember the kind of experience you REALLY want and REALLY deserve. And remember that your mind is very powerful.

I will be visiting soon, as you know, and holding an Intensive in your area. Let me know how this experiment is going and feel free to bring the perceiver (attentiveness of mind) to our gathering of Purpose. I am joined with you in this Purpose of forgiveness and complete awareness of this Purpose is inevitable. I Love You!!!

Love always, David

Approaching the Atonement

Dear David,

Jesus says in the Last Judgment, "Just as the separation occurred over many millions of years, the Last Judgment will extend over a similarly long period, and perhaps an even longer one." Last Judgment meaning man finally judges himself as forgiven and sees himself as God does. Does this mean the healing of the whole Sonship will take many millions of years?

When I look at my own journey I see how rigidly I hold my perceptions in place and how seeing differently can seem to take enormous persuasion and the times that I have got a glimmering that my seeing was wrong and what the truth really was seemed like it was a grain of sand of change that occurred. And I think it took all those years just to have that tiny glimmering. I think I am going to need millions of years to see completely differently to shift my perceptions so wholly! This really freaked me out because I really thought "Wow cool! I really have the solution finally so all I have to do is read it and hey presto my life will change and everything will be wonderful." Now I'm seeing how much it took just to see differently that tiny bit and I am disappointed that I won't have enough time to get it in this life time! I do believe in reincarnation but who wants to go through more death experiences. I have become very disheartened by this.

Can you help?

Hello Beloved One,

Thanks for sharing what is on your heart. Do not be disheartened by the thought of time, for the world you perceive was over long ago. This world is the past. It was just a symbol and represents only the meaning that was given it. It seemed to last but an instant and was forgiven immediately by the Holy Spirit. Process is a time concept, and miracles are simply a gentle use of time to collapse time while you still believe in it. In this sense, time is under the control of the miracle worker. Christ arranges time and space for the miracle worker as the miracle worker seems to perform miracles, and Atonement is the first and last miracle, the Alpha and Omega, and all

the miracles which seemed to come in between. Atonement means Correction and is the awareness that the separation never happened. This cannot be difficult to accept, for no illusion can stand in the Light of Truth. Do not be discouraged by the "process" of Awakening, because all thoughts of "process" are transitory metaphors that simply disappear in the twinkling of an eye. Truth is true and has no exceptions. There was never a time when illusions could replace truth, and time cannot replace Eternity. Spirit and time cannot be reconciled, for Spirit is true and time does not exist. Awakening is nothing more than THIS realization.

Life is neither of the body nor in a body. Life is an Eternal State of Mind. There is no death, for nothing real can die. Forgiveness shows the falsity of illusion and thus makes way for the remembrance of God and Christ. Christ is not born and does not die, remaining Eternal as God created Christ in Spirit. If you seem to be discouraged by judging "progress" remember the teaching of Christ: "Judge not, lest ye be judged." Time is self-judgment, and the Holy Spirit's only use of time is to teach that there is no time.

These words witness to this simple fact. For Christ is fact, and time and Christ cannot co-exist. It only takes one instant for Atonement, yet this instant is without an opposite and thus is completely Certain. Miracles will seem to build your trust, yet Atonement is a moment of complete trust that yields to Absolute Certainty. You cannot fail to accept what is inevitable, and God's Plan for Salvation IS inevitable. Innocence is our Birthright, and nothing can change what God created Perfect and Eternal.

In these writings I use many symbols and metaphors. These are transitory illusions that point beyond themselves. "What Is" is literally beyond symbols and metaphors. Complete forgiveness rendered time past and gone. I rejoice in the Holy Instant and ask but that Christ be glorified by recognizing the Self God created forever Pure and Innocent. In this recognition is God Glorified. All Glory to God forever and ever!

Amen.

ARE WE HERE TO GROW?

Hi David,

Thanks for such a great web site. I have really enjoyed it and appreciate the fact that it is free. I have really learned a lot about the Course from it, especially from the videos with your glowing presence. I have a question about the growth of our spirit or the evolution of spirit, the evolution of consciousness, the evolution of the soul. Whatever symbol you throw out there to describe the eternal part of our identity. The part that is the "I AM" or the Universal Oneness.

I have read quite a bit from Marianne Williamson's books and have read Eckhart Tolle's The Power of Now and now Seth Speaks by Jane Roberts. In all of these books, and I consider these writers to be fairly enlightened (as I do you), they talk about the evolution of soul/spirit/I AM. They talk about the spirit or the I AM on a continuum of growth. Marianne calls it "growing into our perfection" which seems to be a paradox. I am really stuck on this issue and have read your material as well. The material on "no social causes" and how "the soul is change-less." Seth talks about the I AM never being stagnant. That the I AM or the All There Is must create/co-create. It cannot sit bored for it is the most powerful force in the universe and must manifest. It wishes to create form (to manifest itself in form), to express itself creatively through art, teaching and healing. It wants to be aware of itself in form, to create form from thought, create worlds, to grow through a process of happy joy and finally to create even outside of form, to create in all kinds of new ways that we are not even aware of right now.

All of these writers talk about this evolution of the I AM. That some individuals have "progressed" to much higher states of reality where they have much more power and fewer limitations yet are still involved in challenging work. It doesn't seem logical that the I AM would not want to create. That the I AM would just sit still and do nothing. Once we become aware, once we break through the illusion of time/space are we going to do anything? Are growth and creation over? Are there no more challenges?

I asked that my purpose be revealed to me and part of what came back said "your purpose is to grow and experience new things." It seems to me that these writers are saying that the soul, the I AM, will manifest itself in a continuous way and choose to go down infinite paths of infinite possibilities. I know that Marianne has read the Seth material and it has been very influential in her life. The Course says that the body does have a purpose. That it was set up as a learning device. That it was set up as a means of communication. It seems to be a tool for further development not something to attack or dismiss as an illusion only. The body seems to be a valid tool that we chose to use to get experience we couldn't get in other ways. In fact, this earthly reality/existence, even though illusion, seems to be quite valid as a learning environment even though it is not the ultimate I AM or who I really am. It is what I am experiencing right now however. It is a manifestation of my creative thought. It points to what I AM thinking. It is quite valid as is every type of experience and reality.

However, it is all in how I perceive it. Do I perceive it/create it through my true nature? Do I perceive/create the Happy Dream, the Real World or am I stuck only in my five senses. This planet seems to be a process of growth. Even in the Happy Dream we still seem to be growing. I still question. I still read. I still pray. I still do God's will. I fulfill my function here as a teacher in this Happy Dream. The more I teach the more advanced I get according to the Course. It talks about the advanced teachers. We are here to learn things obviously. We are here to learn to love, to learn to forgive. We are here to make this world work. To learn to create with the power of our thoughts, worlds that work. Worlds where love reigns supreme in actuality (in form). To co-create with God who is really ME. It all starts with me. I am the most creative force in this universe. I haven't even begun to tap into my potential. My potential is literally staggering as is the potential of all of my other brethren (for we are all One). The transformation of this world is possible. We are to learn that we can do it. We are to learn that we can work as a team of awake, aware loving Gods.

Most humans we know have not learned these lessons yet. Maybe there have been others before us who HAVE and who are now advanced to other realities. Maybe they are helping us now. Seth talks about coming back into flesh as many times as needed to advance to the next level (a type of reincarnation but not really since Seth agrees with the Course in that there is no time). Seth describes a situation where we are living many lives at once in a multi-dimensional reality but most of us are stuck in the ego and five senses and are not aware of the multi-dimensions. The Course does not throw out the idea of reincarnation and even states that it may be helpful to some people. Could it not be possible that what we think of as the Holy Spirit or God may just be beings who have become aware and have advanced beyond our level and are now acting as our guides. I think being stuck in the old Christian concept of God can create a lot of limitations.

Anyway, sorry this is so rambling. I just had to get it all out. I would love to hear your thoughts about the above information and whether or not you have read the above material/books. I find the question fascinating, yet quite advanced and beyond my current level to understand even though I believe the spirit did tell me that part of my purpose here is to "grow and experience new things." By the way, the other part said my purpose was to "love and teach."

Love

Beloved One,

Thanks for expressing your desire to Wake Up to Eternity. Many seeming stepping stone concepts, including "process" and "evolution" and "reincarnation" are included in the belief in time. The belief in simultaneous time is another step and this includes the Happy Dream of non-judgment. Atonement is the experience that recognizes that the separation never happened. The Big Leap (Enlightenment) is a State of Being which knows no opposite.

Divine Purpose is one with the experience of inner peace, and with the Holy Spirit's Help you will be able to discern the Holy Spirit's Purpose from the ego's purpose. This leads to a decision, or final acceptance of the Correction to the belief in separation. "Growing into our perfection" seems to be a paradox only because of the belief in linear time. In the Holy Instant there is no linear time, for Truth is wholly Present. Time and Eternity do not co-exist, and Awakening is simply the acceptance of the Reality of Eternity.

Creation is Pure Spirit and as Christ says in the Beyond All Idols section of ACIM: "God knows not form." (T-30.III.4) Creation is One Mind. There are no levels or dimensions or degrees or intervals in What Is Forever One. Forgiveness, which is still perceptual, has no levels or individuals. The Happy Dream is unified. In the Happy Dream there are no separate beings, for the tapestry of time/space is one illusion.

If you read carefully through the writings I share you will also notice that "manifesting" is simply another stepping stone concept. What is One simply Is and has no opposite. "To teach" is another way of saying "to think," and forgiveness is simply a complete transformation of thought. Teaching, like prayer, is continuous and not an "event" or "activity." Nothing is personal in forgiveness, and it is apparent that there is only mind. There is not both the mental and the physical because there are no problems apart from the mind. The only sickness was the belief in mind that separation from God was possible. In Waking this belief is Corrected, and only Eternity can be Known. Truth remains forever true.

Happy Waking Beloved One!

Love, David

Releasing Betrayal and Deception

Hello David,

I was at the Gathering in Orlando, FL, at Christ Church Unity. Very Beautiful… I walked away feeling at Peace… I have a question in which I would like your insight… Please… I am having difficulty coming to Peace with my husband's leaving my 9 year old son and I and going off with another woman who he is now married to, after our divorce.

In the beginning my mantra was "I choose Peace instead of this" and I was handling it for awhile… then I just fell apart, and I feel more stable now but still have stuff I know I need to let go of…

Can you give me a way to let go of my ego's hold of his betrayal, deception, breaking of vows, hurtful threats… I realize the deeper the attachment the deeper the letting go… Please Help!!!

Thanks for any help you can give me…

Beloved One,

Thanks for opening up and sharing what is on your mind. Aligning with the ego in any regard always invites the illusion of hurt to make itself at home in an illusion of self. Hurt always comes from the belief that something of the world can bring lasting peace and happiness or take it away. Divorce and marriage are terms that refer to separation and union respectively. True Union is the Christ Mind in Union with the Mind of God and is literally All That Is, far beyond the illusion of time-space. Think of forgiveness as representing Union on earth and special relationships as representing Hell on earth.

Christ devotes 9 chapters (from the end of Ch 15 to the beginning of Ch 24) in ACIM to learning to distinguish between the ego's purpose for relationship and the Holy

Spirit's Purpose. The ego sponsors special relationships to maintain itself, and the Holy Spirit offers the holy relationship as a safe substitute for what the ego made. Betrayal, deception, breaking of vows, hurtful threats are experiences of the special love relationship and the desire for somebody outside of mind to fulfill and make oneself whole. Trust that when one door seems to close another opportunity to forgive is presented.

What you have written reflects the way the Awakening seems to go: "I realize the deeper the attachment, deeper is the letting go." The Holy Spirit would have you realize that peace and happiness and love and joy and freedom are not circumstance dependent. Ego attachment will never satisfy, and with each letting go the awareness of the Truth within comes closer. Be happy for the release of attachment, for you shall know the Truth and in Truth You are free as the Christ. Teach this in every seeming situation, in countless opportunities, and the realization will dawn – I am still as God created Me. Love does not possess. Love has no object. These are the simple lessons Salvation teaches, for Divine Love knows Eternity and has no limits or conditions on Its Giving and Receiving.

Be grateful for every emotion and belief that is flushed up, for nothing real veils the Love of God. As the ego is exposed it becomes apparent that the special relationship offers nothing and the holy relationship always offers a reflection of the Kingdom of Heaven. Aspire only to holy relationship and pray to release all grievances that block the Light from awareness. Offer this blessing to everyone, including your former husband, and you will feel the blessing in your heart. Forgiveness is always a gift to our Self for it releases the illusions of an ego self that could never be. You are deeply Loved, Beloved One.

Love & Blessings abound, David

Beyond the Body is Abstract Light

Dear David,

Blessings to you! Can you please explain the phrase "We cannot even think of God without thinking of a body?" From my happy experience when I think of my brothers it seems their body separates and I find them with me and Jesus, sitting together looking at what is going on with us as bodies… I am not sure of this thought… but when I think like this it seems that I join with them in a happy setting… what could this thought be leading to? How could I sustain this thought? Thanks for looking into it with me.

Love always.

Greetings Beloved One,

Thanks for writing. When the mind seemed to fall asleep and forget the Abstract Light of Heaven, the ego projected a cosmos of specifics to take the place of, or substitute for Divine Abstraction. To the mind that believes it is in time-space, Abstraction has been completely forgotten or blocked from awareness. All that the deceived mind perceives is forms and specifics, and this is why it cannot think of God without thinking of a body. After the great amnesia, form became the "known" and the Abstract Light of Heaven became the "unknown."

Forgiveness turns the mind back toward the Light and returns the experience of causation to the mind, which alone is causative. The symbol of bodies together is a stepping stone, for truly bodies cannot join. It is the Purpose of the Holy Spirit in the mind which is the joining, and this Purpose sustains peace of mind. With this Purpose comes the Happy Dream, for one dreams softly of a sinless world in a unified perception. The tapestry is One, and all is well.

Love always, David

BLESSINGS AND SYMBOLS

Hi David,

My husband and myself are now surfing the internet; just an out picturing of the Mind, and boy are we having fun! It is still all pretty new but I'm getting the hang of it. We were married on New Year's Day! Yeah! We married on Jan. 1, the first day of the first month at 11:11.

All symbolic of starting over at the beginning. New Birth! New purpose for relationship! Holy Relationship! Anyway, Blessings to you in the new year! In the Real Sense, we are all married in God! We are eternal partners in the dance!

I still would like to come and do some recording. I will know when the time is right. I want to do a children's album which might need to happen here, because I want to use some of the children who are so talented in the child care centers I work at. I might even do a video with them. We went to Owensboro for Christmas. It was Great. Got Rachel a car. She will be starting Community College this semester.

Love

Thanks Beloved One,

I rejoice with you in our Eternal Union! The symbols of the One abound! You are always welcome in my Heart. Send me a copy of the album and/or video when it comes through. It is always a joy hearing from you.

Love always, David

Chapter 2

CAN WE FORM A RELIGION BASED ON ACIM?

David,

In 1980 I came across A Course in Miracles. I remember starting to read the Text. All the words made sense. There was a spiritual message in every sentence of every paragraph and in every chapter. I read with caution, as I expected at any moment the story line would change and there would be some weird cosmology or a fearless leader to follow. It was with great relief when I finished all three books and found them to be a meaningful and coherent spiritual path.

The Course is a pure spiritual path of itself. It has the single purpose of teaching us the complete escape from fear. But experience has shown me that the students of the Course are not as single minded. Almost everyone new to the Course comes with expectations of how to improve relationships and career, make more money, learn new healing techniques, and make new friends. It is the pursuit of "worldly healing" which has fractured the Course community. It is my belief that the Course community needs to come together and formally organize a religion based on A Course in Miracles.

The key to the Course is the holy instant. The holy instant is a brief moment, experienced in time but stepping out of time to remember our True Self.

To properly use this key, we simply practice the holy instant as often and frequently as we possibly can, when we awake, all through our day, and when we retire at night. In each practice of the holy instant, a miracle is born into the world. The more we practice the holy instant, the more miracles there are linking each moment to the next, until our minds experience the Atonement, the continual practice.

People need to see what the Bible really has to say, in its own words. The real message of the Bible is that treachery is good when used for ourselves, that God favors a few over the many, that big shepherd families need choice lands belonging to others, and that war is a suitable means for taking that land. The Bible tells the story of how Moses and his forefathers were given the land of Canaan by God, yet they had to raise an army and destroy its inhabitants in complete genocide to effect God's will.

We must get the word out. We must call out the need to search for truth. We take for granted that the world has the Internet, freedom of speech, and freedom of religion. But this is it. This is the big break humanity has been waiting for. We have the spiritual teaching of ACIM, we have the means for positive and meaningful change. It would be a tragedy indeed to get this far and not take advantage of this incredible opportunity

Beloved Child of God,

Thanks for your devotion to Awakening. It is always a blessing to seek the Lord with all your heart and soul and might, and what one seeks within one will find. Religion is experience and the experience of peace is natural for a Child of God, yet it must be uncovered and discovered if it seems to be beyond awareness. Religion is truly the experience of the Holy Instant, the Present Moment, for what time but Now can Truth be known. Now is the only time there is.

If you read lesson #135 in the Workbook of ACIM you see that defensiveness arises with the attempt to plan the future, acti-vate the past, or organize the present. Religion is experience,

never theology or doctrine or ritual, and the experience of the Present Moment cannot be organized. When Christ says "the Kingdom of Heaven is at hand" and "the Kingdom of Heaven is Now" and "the Kingdom of Heaven is within," this refers to the Present Moment, the Holy Instant. The Present is before time was, and this is the meaning of the statement: "Before Abraham was, I am."

History would not seem to exist unless the same mistake was repeated over and over. Atonement shows that the "mistake" of separation was never real and therefore has had no effect on Reality. It is impossible for that which never happened to change God's Love, Which is forever Real and True.

I love You forever and ever, David

CAUSE AND EFFECT

David,

Thank you so much for your help. I wonder if you could kindly elaborate on the thought expressed in the section titled Healing as Release from Fear that says that "it can be believed (erroneously) that the mind can miscreate in the body, or that the body can miscreate in the mind. I realize that the body does not create… but I don't understand the words… that "the mind can miscreate in the body."

Is it another way of saying that fearful thoughts create disease in the body. And what would be an example of believing that the body can miscreate in the mind.

With gratitude.

Beloved One,

Thanks for your questions. Yes, you are on the right track. It can be believed erroneously that the mind can miscreate in the body, and this is the attempt to project guilt onto the body. But since ideas leave not their source, it is the sleeping mind which continues to retain the guilt. Until the sleeping mind forgives, it cannot "get rid of" guilt. Through the attempt to project guilt the mind keeps it. Projection is really a defense mechanism through which the ego keeps the mind feeling guilty.

An example of believing that the body can miscreate in the mind is the belief that behaviors and actions can damage the mind. The thoughts: "your behavior has harmed your son's mind" or "those violent behaviors in that TV show can damage your child's mind" are two examples of this.

Behavior is never causative, being a byproduct of thought. What you do comes from what you think. The lesson of forgiveness teaches that only mind is causative and that mind cannot create beyond itself. Mind reaches to itself. It does not go out. Within itself is everything, you within it and it within you. There is nothing else. Atonement shows that You are a Divine Mind, wholly Mind, and Purely Mind. You remain forever an Idea in the Mind of God. The Christ Idea!

All Glory to the Living God, and thanks be to God for creating Christ Perfect, Eternal, and Free in Spirit. Amen.

Love, David

INSIGHT ABOUT THE DREAM

Dear David,

I just finished reading Chapters 27-29 of ACIM. The chapters refer to "dreams" and the "gap." There appears to be a little confusion concerning the following:

Everything outside of us is a dream that we (dreamers) made. Thus the entire cosmos is a dream we made. Yet the dream is nothing (illusion). Then ACIM discusses how to approach (forgive) your brother by not accepting his dream (sickness). If your brother appears to be in your dream then he is an illusion. Perhaps the brother appears in your dream the way you perceive him, yet he is also the Son of God (which is beyond the perception/ dream). So forgiving your brother who appears to be attacking you is the same as forgiving yourself because you still perceive "attack" outside of you, which means that "fear" or "the gap" is still there (within). Is that a correct interpretation of ACIM?

I would appreciate if you could share your insight about these chapters. I want to awake from the "dream." I want to let go of all illusions just like letting go of a pencil out your hand (I am very desirous). I want to be healed so that I can heal others.

Gratefully yours with everlasting love, Holy One

Beloved of God,

Thanks for your devotion to Awakening. The gap of time-space is all that needs be overlooked or forgiven. This was a gap believed to be between Cause (God) and Effect (Christ). Yet as Jesus said, I and the Father are One. There is no gap in what is an Eternal, Real Relationship of Pure Spirit. The illusory gap of separation seemed to

project a script of bodies, each going their own separate ways. In sleep, "minds" seem walled off by flesh, alone and isolated. Forgiveness recognizes mind as one and therefore overlooks the belief in private minds and private thoughts. Sickness is literally an impossible thought because it has no "source" and cannot be shared. Only the Mind of God can be shared, for such is Creation.

Forgiveness opens the door to Self-realization, for forgiveness sees that there is nothing "outside" of mind. Mind reaches to itself, it does not go out. It encompasses you entirely. Within itself is everything, you within it and it within you. There is nothing else anywhere or ever. True empathy means sharing or extending only what is true, for only Truth can be shared. False empathy is the erroneous attempt to share a concept that God did not create. God did not create the concept of sickness and so it cannot be shared. There is only one dreamer and this is why you are asked to join the dreamer and not the dream.

The dream of bodies cannot be joined, and bodies do not join. The body was made as a concrete symbol of separation, yet given to the Holy Spirit it serves solely as a means or symbol of communication. In Enlightenment; the recognition of the Pure Oneness of Mind, the body has no Purpose because it has no existence. At no single instant does the body exist at all. The body is always remembered or anticipated but never Present. This means that the body is an illusory time-based concept.

Illusions are one and so forgiveness lets them all go together. This has been stated many ways, i.e., there is only one problem that is already solved. No hierarchy of illusions. No order of difficulty in miracles. Atonement is complete forgiveness. It sees that the separation from God never happened. Forgiveness is Still and quietly does nothing. It looks and watches and judges not. Such is healing. Such is mind at rest.

Blessings of Love, David

CHRISTIAN SCIENCE AND
A COURSE IN MIRACLES

David,

I was interested in the course many years ago, but drifted away. Since then I have become a devout Christian Scientist. It seems the two are in many ways similar, and I feel that studying the course might make me a better Christian Scientist. Do you have any thoughts on this? I have always thought studying CS would help anyone, no matter what path they choose. I just do not want to get into the course again and find out that it is not compatible with Mary Baker Eddy's teachings. Christian Science is my life, along with my pug dog Baxter.

Beloved One,

Thanks for your e-mail and for your devotion to Awakening. The Holy Spirit is Guiding you to an experience. Let the Holy Spirit within Guide your approach to this experience. Christian Science and ACIM are reflections of the same Divine Principle, inspired by the same Source. Let your goal be forgiveness, Awakening to God's Love, and trust that the seeming tools and symbols of the moment are the Holy Spirit's gifts to you to use as Guided. Form will always seem to vary until Atonement is accepted, for Atonement is the Content that shows the meaninglessness of the concept of "different forms."

Illusions are one and are therefore the same. Books and paths seem to be separate forms until the goal they point to is recognized. Let the Holy Spirit lead you to the happy realization that there are not "two" to compare :)
Blessings of Love!

In Peace, David

CLARIFICATION ABOUT THE BIBLE

Hi David,

I know you said you would be away for a couple of weeks. I have been reading many things on the Awakening mind site, and the Group. After reading many of your writings I'm wondering… I believe the Bible is the inspired Word of God. I have read your writings, and I have been Blessed by your writings, but I'm wondering… the Bible clearly talks about Heaven and Hell. And I know universal Atonement & forgiveness is for everyone. I believe the words of the Bible are not man's words but the Bible is Inspired by God. So I believe everything is true.

The Bible talks about Jesus returning for his Elect. And we ultimately make the choice to Receive or reject God and Salvation – The Finished Work of Atonement. He Draws us – we do have free will and we can choose not to respond. God did not create us as robots. I want to understand. Those that are killing and murdering and continuing in this and will not receive God's Atonement – will they be in Heaven or awaken to Heaven? I know you say heaven is now and the Holy Instant is now

God drew me to Himself. I was on the way to a health store. And it was not open yet. And a young lady was talking about my salvation that instant. I was awakened from the slumber – it was like a light came on. I do go to a Church & fellowship and I will continue to walk in love & light. When I read your writings I feel love and Joy but then I don't understand many things. The bible says heaven and earth will pass away but my Word will not pass away.

What about the Gospel being preached for every nation? If Heaven is now and we can live in a heavenly state now, why does it say God will return for his elect? The Bible makes it clear not everyone will receive salvation. God does not force us to worship him. I know it's not God's will that any man should perish. Are we not accountable for our actions and reap what we sow. From what I read on your site I'm questioning everything.

So when I wake up and see the clouds and see my family and go outside that is not real. Everything I see I know is temporal and fleeting. And you said there is no time. God created time, did He not, for us? I know He exists in eternity. Does God not communicate with us through his Holy Spirit according to our understanding?

Sin is not real and yet there is atonement for it. The world is dark – is the light in our vessels? Are we not the Light of the world and we are to carry salvation to others who have not awakened to the Truth? Please can you clarify, Brother. Everything is being shaken to me. God Is. Period. But what I'm reading, It rocks Everything. Please, what I have written is honest and I know you will answer from Truth and your heart.

Peace and Blessings.

Dear Beloved One,

Thanks for your heartfelt and sincere questions. The Bible can be a very helpful tool for accepting Atonement or Salvation. The Inspiration you speak of is the Word of God or the Spirit of God, and the Word is ever available to the soul that is open and willing and ready. Scripture is intended to offer a way to accept Atonement or complete forgiveness, and thus to remember our Eternal Union with God.

The Holy Spirit interprets Scripture for this Purpose: Awakening to the Truth. This was expressed in the Gospels as "I and my Father are One" and "You shall know the truth and the truth shall set you free." Heaven is the State of our Eternal Union, or the Truth of our Being, and the closest approximation of Heaven with regard to earth is Now. This is the Meaning of: "The Kingdom of Heaven is at hand." Heaven is not a place or a location, but Heaven is a State of Mind (Being in Perfect Peace & Happiness). Heaven is Eternal and God's Word (Spirit) is Eternal and shall never pass away. The cosmos of planets and stars, earth, time, space, etc. are temporal and shall pass away.

"Satan" and "hell" and "sin" describe the condition of the belief in separation from God – the so-called "fall" from Grace. God is Love and in Truth Love has no opposite. This was expressed in the Bible as: "Perfect Love casts out fear." The tree of the knowledge of good and evil in Genesis represents the belief in duality, and taking a bite from this tree is symbolic of attempting the impossible. For God is Pure Love and Oneness, and duality is literally impossible. The world perceived through the five senses is a dream that the separation from God actually happened, and the Bible says that Adam fell asleep. At no point in the Bible is it written that Adam (representing human beings) woke up, yet the Gospels clearly reveal that Jesus Awoke to the Truth of Reality: "The Kingdom of Heaven is within" and "My Kingdom is not of this world" and "Before Abraham was, I am." Christ is Mind Awake, the I Am Presence, the Identity which God Creates forever in the Mind of God.

Atonement is the Correction to the seeming error of separation from God, and as you have written "universal Atonement & forgiveness is for everyone." The idea of "Jesus returning for his Elect" needs a slight modification to be meaningful. The mind which elected to accept the Correction "returned for Christ Elect" or remembered ItSelf as the Christ, the Eternal Child of God. Jesus demonstrated this decision for everyone, voluntarily electing to accept the Correction and remember Christ's Origin in God. This decision is truly the only decision that can be shared, for in Truth it is impossible to turn away from or be separate from God. This is why there is no "eternal hell," for mistaken identity has been Corrected by the Holy Spirit, and Awakening is simply a matter of accepting this Atonement.

God Wills Spirit in Heaven forever, and so Spirit Is. God does Communicate with you through the Holy Spirit according to your understanding. Since you perceive your brothers and sisters in form in your awareness, it will be meaningful to say to you that everyone will accept this Correction in due time for it is a decision that is literally impossible to reject. The Love of God is All-Inclusive and has nothing to do with the ego concept of rejection. Love is Total Inclusion and error has no meaning to Love. God did not create time, and so Awakening in Christ requires seeing the impossibility of linear time. In the Holy Instant there is no time, for the Present Moment is the Gateway to Eternity.

The Bible says: "As you sow, so shall you reap." This scripture is with reference to thoughts, and it is thoughts which motivate actions. "Blessed are the pure of heart for they shall see God" refers to purity of thought. "Judge not, lest you be judged" means that the mind can elect a state of forgiveness or nonjudgment and reminds that any judgment the mind makes is made on itself. The incentive for freedom and peace of mind is therefore to be without judgment.

This is the simple approach to Awakening in Christ. To teach is to demonstrate, so "the Gospel being preached to every nation" is meaningfully interpreted as demonstrating the Unconditional Love of God to everyone by example in thought, word, action, and attitude. This is also what it means to be the Light of the world.

The temporal shall pass away, yet the Eternal shall last forever. This is the meaning of Awakening in Christ.

Beloved Child of God, there is another web site that will help deepen your understanding of the ideas I speak about as you allow the Holy Spirit to interpret the Bible's Scriptures in the Great Awakening. You will be Guided to many verses of Biblical Scripture and Given the stepping stones to the Kingdom of Heaven within. I will meet You there, for our Identity is the same in Christ and Christ abides in Eternity. The website is www.the-christ.net.

Be blessed with every seeming step you take, for the Holy Spirit's Guidance is sure. I am with you always, even unto the end of time. Amen.

Forever in Love, David

COMING TO TRUE PERCEPTION

My question is about a discrepancy between Marianne Williamson's audio tape on a Course in Miracles and what I have been learning from the Course in Miracles. In my job, occasionally it falls to me to enforce minor laws and morals. It seems the Course in Miracles repeats over and over again that anything that is not eternal is simply not real and if I understand correctly part of a miracle is over-looking all errors and allowing the Holy Spirit to fill your mind with more true perception.

In Marianne Williamson's audio tapes she says that when someone commits a crime that would entail the person going to jail, that they would still go to jail but the miracle she offers is changing the perception of jails, from being how they are seen now to seeing them as places of healing and learning. But I have noticed that it takes hundreds of hours of thinking about someone's crime to enforce even a minor offence. And like the Course says, you give to yourself whatever you think of another person. I find that when I spend time thinking about what other people may have done wrong, I do tend to think that other people are projecting negative ideas on to me.

Thanks, blessings.

Beloved One,

Thanks for writing. Forgiveness is always a gift to our Self because it releases the make-believe self/world/cosmos of the ego and opens the way to remembrance of Self and God. As a brother or sister is recognized beyond the body, their Innocence as a Divine Creation is recognized. You have written that the "miracle is over-looking all errors..." and this is so. With the Help of the Holy Spirit it is possible to look beyond error to the Light of the Atonement, Which is forever Innocent and Sinless. Pardon is always justified because the misperceptions of the ego are not real.

The Golden Rule asks you to do unto others as you would have others do unto you. See no body as guilty and you see nobody to blame. The Innocence of the Spirit is apparent when one realizes that attack is impossible. A unified mind cannot attack or be attacked. And without the belief in attack guilt has no basis. The Holy Spirit gently leads to a unified mind and a unified perception that is the forgiven world. When forgiveness has been accepted, the illusion of guilt has vanished from awareness.

It is possible to perceive any seeming situation as extending Love or Calling for Love. Let the Holy Spirit show you by aligning your mind with this Guidance. Healing is unlearning the ego and thus releasing every scrap of ego belief, thought, emotion, and perception. If you are willing the way will open, for nothing can obscure the Innocence the Holy Spirit would have you behold.

Love, David

CROSSING THE BARRIER TO PEACE

Blessed Brother David,

I just finished reading several of the archived messages. What a blessing from Spirit. I wrote you last year when I was out of work and concerned for my family. My wife and I had sent in the rent check trusting that Holy Spirit would provide. Someone who reads these messages was led to offer assistance to us, and I found employment shortly thereafter.

A few months ago I was laid off yet again and we have felt the strain. One of the sisters wrote you expressing a feeling of which I can relate. In my attempts at giving this over to Spirit I find myself struggling in part because I not only don't know what to do, I don't know exactly how, or what to pray about in this situation.

I can't seem to find a position that I can have peace with. I can't pray for a place where I "fit in," because I know that this is not my home and this world is an illusion. I can't really ask for satisfying employment because in awakening I find that nothing here can satisfy. Still, I wish to be useful and of course there is the appearance of having a wife, three teens, two dogs, a cat, a car payment, the apparent "need" to eat, etc...

I do understand that we cannot "ask the impossible," which of course means that we all go together or not at all and I do feel compassion for our brothers and sisters, but I do so long for peace. I want to go home. I don't think I've ever really felt at home here in this illusionary world. I have always felt out of place somehow. I have also felt like I was failing in life, unworthy and undeserving, cursed even, comparatively.

A few years ago my second wife left me when my three children from my first failed marriage came to live with us. I was devastated. I longed for physical death. Anything to ease what was really the culmination of a lifetime of misery. My physical father was a gay man with an alcohol problem who left when I was six. My bodily mother was and is paranoid/schizophrenic and I was the oldest of two boys so I received the brunt of it… I was molested by my Southern Baptist Sunday School teacher when I was twelve and thirteen. This was a man I had trusted and looked up to. I repressed the memory for nearly twenty years. And on and on. This dream has seemed like a nightmare at times for me. Oh and my physical brother seemed to be blessed in every way, not just spared somehow, but just unbelievably blessed.

I realize this is all illusion now and forgive me for going on. I am blessed having gone through the night. You and this group are a miracle to me. My beloved wife is a miracle. I've had this block to my experience of peace regarding the appearance of lack. So I've been trying to give it over to Spirit and I remembered the story of the children of Israel apparently being trapped before an impassible barrier at the Red Sea and how it took a miracle for them to cross over so they could continue their journey.

I've been hoping to find the right job and experience prosperity and peace; to get un-stuck so I could move on in my journey. Last night I couldn't sleep. As I lay there the Holy Spirit revealed something to me. He showed me that the real barrier to the awareness of Love's Presence for me was my unforgiveness of all the shadow figures in my life, my seeming abusers and abandoners, myself for "failing" and for blaming God. I know I can't forgive this by myself. I need help to cross this block to peace. I thank Holy Spirit. Although I still feel some inner conflict I know that the source of my guilt/fear pain is within and therefore so is my salvation. I feel as if I am standing on the edge of a cliff and I need Holy Spirit's help to take the next step.

I would appreciate your prayers and guidance. Also for my wife who desperately needs an operation which we can't afford and my three beautiful children who have been through their own ringer. Thank you my brother. I am not afraid.

Peace and Love.

Dear Beloved One,

Thanks for pouring your heart out and being open and willing for Guidance about prayer. You and Janie and your family are in my thoughts and prayers.

Now for some Guidance about prayer. Prayer is desire. A heart which knows no desire has cleared the Altar of mind and desires that there be no idols before God. Desirelessness is Completion, and God created Christ Whole and Complete. Desirelessness means that there is nothing to add or wish or want beyond the Perfection that God Gives Eternally. Single or Unified desire is Creation, and this is the meaning of "Let Thine Eye be Single."

As the Altar of mind is made clean, freed from the desire for the impossible, the Memory of God will return to awareness.

Release the past, for it is gone. No longer seek to repeat what is already over and gone. Prayer for specifics asks that the past be repeated in some form that the mind believes is desirable. Desirelessness is of the Present Moment, this Holy Instant. Be Content with what is forever Real and True. God Gives only Love.

Love & Blessings forever and ever, David

DAVID, IS IT REAL?

David,

Forgiveness offers me everything that I want. These thoughts came today.

It is real that forgiving the world is forgiving myself? Forgiving my own making? So as I forgive the world I am forgiving myself? Is it real, that I can look at everything in this world, with no judgment or attachment, knowing that everything that exists is love? So I can be happy, in peace and certain? Is it really that God has chosen us to share his vision, heal ourselves, heal brothers, bringing his light, being at one with Him and with our brothers? Are our brothers ourselves? Is it real that this is our journey back home, his plan, my path of salvation, a journey back home to Heaven? Is it real that just my willingness for truth and faith replaces all errors in my mind? That Holy Spirit guides us and that there is no effort or doing from our part? Was this experience somewhat similar with you? I would love to hear some depth in this regard from you.

Love

Beloved One of God,

Yes my dear brother in Christ, forgiveness offers everything that you want!

As you forgive the ego self that could never be, you have also forgiven the world. God did not create the world and so it must be forgiven or overlooked, so that the Spirit which God creates can be recognized and experienced. As you forgive you can look at everything in this world, with no judgment or attachment, knowing that everything that exists is Love. In this you can be happy, in peace, and certain. As you forgive, you understand that God has chosen you to share His Vision

and Be a bringer of Light, Being at One with Him and with our brothers. As you forgive, you see that everyone shares the same Self, One Mind. As you forgive you see that this is our journey back Home, His Plan, our path of Salvation, a journey without distance back Home to Heaven, our Eternal Love in God.

It is true that just a little willingness for Truth and faith replaces all errors in the mind. The Holy Spirit Guides with certainty and gentleness and you need but be willing to move in the direction of Truth. Yes, this is my experience, and I share it fully with you in the Holy Spirit. No one can fail who seeks to know the Truth of this experience. You can feel the Guidance carrying you along to a certain inward Destination. Every seeming step will grow in confidence, for one is never alone on this journey. God is inevitable, and nothing can come to keep the mind from the Great Awakening! Let go, surrender, and enjoy the miracles.

Thanks for Answering the Call with a resounding Yes! I look forward to seeing you very soon. Those that have heard the Call and Answered are showing up. They are gathering for the final turns of the seeming script and the way is short Now. We have come together to rejoice in God's Love and Oneness, and in our own Oneness in God. God and Christ share the same Will for Perfect happiness. The time of Heaven is at hand and the celebration is on.

Love, love, love, David

THE DESIRE FOR UNION
IS THE CALL TO REMEMBER GOD

Hello David,

I thank our Father for this web site. I enjoy all the questions as well as the light that is seen in the response. The question on my heart is this: I see that the "ego" brings forth these illusions that think to be a separate thing from One, having a power of itself. When the truth of love is seen fully though, is there such a thing as marriage? A part of me still desires this 'union' but I guess what I am saying is doesn't He place that desire within, but we just see it amiss in separation? And what does this look like in Spirit and in truth?

I am not a student of ACIM, but the eyes have been opened to see what is being said. The things that I have seen, I do agree with, and yet still am not drawn to take the "course" as of this "time." But I see that as irrelevant and I am sure you do also ~smiles~. Would appreciate your sight on this,

Thanks.

Beloved One,

Thanks for your heart felt e-mail. Yes, the desire for union is seen amiss in a world based on separation. In Truth marriage has no form, for marriage is Content in Spirit and in Truth. Marriage is a word that symbolizes the desire for union, and as you approach the Kingdom of Heaven within it becomes apparent that Union is fully and truly experienced as Oneness with God. To know Christ is to know that the Father and I are One. This is the Union of Divine Mind. In this world marriage can be a step toward this Union if the relationship is given to the Holy Spirit to direct. Marriage as the union of partners is an initial com-

mitment that is meant to lead toward the commitment to accept Atonement, to accept the Correction to the belief in separation.

Purpose is always the key: Who is my Guide, remembering that it is impossible to serve two masters? The Holy Spirit uses relationship to heal and bless. The ego uses relationship to make a false idol and to perpetuate itself. In Salvation or Enlightenment the experience is Total Oneness. It is not really that two become One, but rather that Union is the Being of Oneness God creates Eternally. God placed the desire to Awaken on your heart, and this is the Call to remember God. The Holy Spirit is this Call and thus the Holy Spirit is your desire for Union. "The Union cannot be experienced in duality, and that is why I am Calling you out of the world – for this is a world of duality." The Union of God and Christ is reflected in the forgiven world, and this is the Atonement.

One outgrows the concept of partnership with a body or soul as one fully accepts and realizes our Divine Union with God. Until the moment of Self-realization there will seem to be the concept of partnership which can be used for a "time," under the Guidance of the Holy Spirit, to lead beyond the belief in time.

Happy marriage Beloved Child of God! Follow as the Holy Spirit directs and let every encounter be a holy encounter.

I love You forever and ever! David

DESIRE IS THE KEY

David,

I have been reading the transcripts from the Argentina gatherings. In one of them you mention your reading ACIM eight hours a day. When you read them so voraciously, were you also absorbing what you read? I also seem to have been searching since I was a child, feeling as if nothing makes sense here, as if I had mistakenly landed on the wrong planet. Neither could I find my "niche," for no role seemed to have eternal validity on which to base its realness.

However, when I am reading ACIM, I sometimes glimpse the truth in it, only to find that it seems as if I can't even remember its content when I read it over again, as if I had absorbed nothing. I just keep reading and doing the workbook, hoping I am connecting on some level. I have got more from your talks in Argentina than I get out of ACIM; however, up to this point the bulk of my unlearning has come from listening to Resta's music nonstop, over and over again. At this rate, she will have to sing the whole ACIM course for me to get understanding and unlearning.

Help!

Beloved One,

By the time I came across ACIM in 1986 I was already immersed in the Spirit and saw ACIM as the answer to a prayer. I resonated with most everything I read in ACIM at that time. When the mind sees the value of what is offered, distractions and investments in concepts of the world fall away quickly. It is really a matter of willingness and desire, for as Jesus says: "No amount of evidence will convince you of what you do not want." (T-16.II.6)

I saw ACIM as my escape from fear, and poured my heart and soul into it. It was more important to me than money, family, friends, even breathing. It is also very simple. That is why I understood what the Course was pointing to – the Present Moment. Only Now is understandable. Be gentle with yourself and fan the flames of your passion to know God and Self. Music will be a big part of your path! Bask in it. Thanks for writing and sharing what is on your heart.

Love Sweet Love, David

Chapter 3

DOES MY BROTHER'S PAIN EXIST?

Dear David,

I have a philosophical issue that has kept me from progressing in my path back to God. It has come up again in my life, so I will illustrate it with the current situation.

Last night, my boyfriend of four years and I broke up. He has had an unusually troubled childhood with a lot of violence and a mother who abused him and then committed suicide when he was a teenager. Because of this, he is a very needy person once you get past his hard exterior. Throughout the relationship I kept believing that I could create a miracle and show him that life is not so sad and scary as he believes. At times it seemed to work, and there were some truly sacred moments. In the end, however, the ego took control, and I felt incapable of seeing past the ugliness and darkness – especially when he seemed to think I was the only bright thing in his life and clung to me for dear life.

Although I've not told anyone yet about the break-up, I'm sure my friends and family will be happy that I "got away" from such a cynical, childish person. But now all I can think is that the things that disgusted me in the end (the dirty house, the dark clinging attitude, the irresponsible behavior, etc.) were really just his belief in the lack of love. And sadly, it was that belief that drove me away. I've failed.

Many months ago, I wrote to you about my concerns about abandoning this person. You said that the falsehood is my belief that I am capable of abandoning another. I have contemplated this idea many times, and I do understand that this person is in God always, as am I, but I also cannot deny the "seeming" pain that he is experiencing by my pulling away from him.

Why is the "seemingness" of things always dismissed in ACIM? If he experiences a "seemingness" of pain, then I don't care if it's not real, it's still cause for my concern! It seems that if I followed the Course principles, I could just go do my lessons and feel happy and loving while he rots in his own self-created hell. Or maybe his pain really doesn't exist on ANY level, and therefore I should just not give a crap about other people's suffering.

I hope you understand the issue I'm trying to get at. Or maybe this is all just ego talk, and I don't even know what I'm saying? I don't know any more. Perhaps you can see through all this better than me.

Thank you so much for your love and patience!

Beloved One,

Thanks for sharing what is on your heart. Your question about the perception of pain is a good starting point in clearing the mirror of the mind. This mirror must be cleared of false beliefs and concepts and thoughts if you are to radiate the Light that is ever Present. Pain is always a misperception, for God has nothing to do with pain. If God is real there is no pain. "If pain is real, there is no God." (W-190.3.4) The illusion of pain always stems from wrong-minded thinking, and this is what must be exposed and released to experience lasting peace and happiness.

Concern is another word for worry, and this emotion has nothing to do with compassion or true empathy. Concern is an emotion that is painful and arises from a desire to be right about a particular person, situation, or event. One aspect of

such concern is the belief that something false has already happened. Another aspect is the belief that past events caused the fear and pain. This misperception gives reality to the past and denies the Present Solution offered by the Holy Spirit. When you pray for a miracle you are praying for a change in your perception. Even when you seem to pray for "another" this is still the case. If you seem to have continuing concern for a brother after asking for a miracle you are not allowing the miracle to be as it is. Miracles do not create or really change; they simply look calmly upon the false and see that it has no consequence. Miracles offer only Joy, and when Joy has come all pain is over Now.

The concept of leaving someone behind is a strange belief, for in God's Love there is no such thing as leaving. The ego is the belief in possession, and what seems capable of being possessed also seems capable of being lost. Loss is the ego's story and originated with the belief that it is possible to separate or "fall" from God's Eternal Love. This error seems to be acted out and repeated in human relationships, just as the past seems to repeat. The miracle Awakens the mind to the awareness that the past is over and only a blessing remains.

Pain is correctly perceived as a Call for Love, and this is always one's own Call to release the false perception of pain. Looking through a glass darkly never brings peace, happiness, love, or joy, so any seeming upset is a Call to empty the mind of false concepts and thus clean the mirror. This is the mind training that is required to accept the Atonement and remember God. Atonement is the awareness that the separation never happened. Until this Correction is accepted the world will seem real and the unreal emotions of the ego that are one with the world will seem to persist in awareness.

Let the feelings come up into awareness. Then, with deep honesty and sincerity, give the thoughts and judgments and interpretations and feelings over to the Spirit.

When darkness is raised to Light the darkness is gone. Do not protect the darkness, for the Spirit will not dissolve what has not been willingly offered for release. You have the Answer within but have been unwilling to let go of the ego definition of the problem. The Holy Spirit must wait until you see that you have had a perception problem based on belief in the ego. Until this point is reached the "problems" will seem to be projected to the world and to brothers that seem apart from the mind. They are not. There are no problems apart from the mind. Healed perception will spring to awareness the instant the misperception is seen exactly as it is and not concealed or projected as "something else."

All illness was mental illness, and all perceived pain was nothing but a faulty formulation of Reality. Reality is Love, and Love is created Eternally Perfect. Love has no opposite.

Glory to God for creating Love as One forever and ever!

Love & Blessings, David

CAN I SIMPLY DROP IT ALL?
DO I NEED TO MAKE IT IN THE WORLD?

E-mail #1

Dear Holy Brother,

According to ACIM (or "Jesus") the ego or the world that is seen outside is all false and unreal, because it never happened. In other words, the Son of God never "fell asleep" and "had a dream" or never separated from God.

Then how is it this seeming world outside that is a projection from within our minds which is all unreal and has no existence can appear?

I understand that we made it (the world outside) to appear real based on error. Also, in ACIM, it mentioned that every time a problem arises we do not look at the problem itself (which will make it "more real") instead we look within. It is like saying if the worldly things including obligations are all unreal, then, we can simply "drop it" or "let go" (let God). It is like saying forget about taxes or bills or the whole world because they are not real. However, in ACIM Jesus teaches or at least mentions how to look (outside or inside) without judgment (because there is nothing to judge).

Please share your kind guidance to clarify this delusion.

E-mail #2

Dear David,

I think I know the answer before I pose the question, but just to clarify my thoughts. I am a student of ACIM. I also have gotten sober over 8 years ago and have been on a spiritual path with inventory process; removal of character defects; making amends etc, all the work necessary for me to become a functioning member of the world. And therein lies my dilemma.

I have been struggling so to become a functioning member of the world because I failed so miserably in it. I threw away money on alcohol and other addictions; I ran through an earthly inheritance from my father; I ran up credit card bills and basically couldn't make a living for myself. I have been working for the past few years with jobs and stand to be able to make a great deal of money in this one particular job; enough to pay off my debts and get me "clear." However, the stress and the physical strain is great on me.

My question is: is the reason I am still struggling with this the fact that I am trying to make it "in this world"? Otherwise I think I would be relaxed and joyful all the time. The fact is I am not as spiritual as I profess to be to the people who know me. I really am still very much on this material realm and don't fully trust as yet. I need any insights you can give. I have gotten much from you over the past few months, David, and really appreciate the time and energy you give.

Thanks.

Dear Beloved One,

Thanks for writing. You are beginning to understand why you cannot judge your "advances" or "retreats," your seeming "successes" and "failures" with regards to this world. This world is backwards and upside down, and nothing in distorted perception is as it seems. I am Calling you out of this upside down world. I am saying that the Kingdom is not of this world. I am not asking you to "be in the world but not of it." Nothing of this world will ever satisfy your holy mind, for this world was made as an attack on God and was made to be a place where God could not enter. This world was made to deny the Truth of Divine Love.

Now the core of Awakening is becoming clear: It is impossible to see two worlds and therefore it is impossible to make it "in the world." You were not created to function in a world of images that God did not create. When you forgive the cosmos you let go of the attempt to reconcile Truth with illusions, Spirit with matter, or Eternity with time. Allow the Holy Spirit to work through and in your mind and it becomes apparent that you have no competing "parts." Forgive and see that all is whole and nothing is apart from mind. From on High there is nothing to do but Observe. This is the meaning of "Above the battleground." (T-23.IV.9). There is no stress or concern or confusion from Above.

Appearances deceive. Nothing of the five senses will lead to Awakening. The five senses serve the ego and were made to report differences. As long as the illusion of judgment persists in awareness, the five senses bring witness to illusory categories that have no meaning and no reality. As judgment fragments perception, forgiveness unifies it. Yet this unification of perception, seeing the wholeness, is a perspective of mind and not a function of the body. Beyond unified perception is the Vision of Christ, Which is not perceptual at all. This Abstract Light can literally be called Seeing or Sight, yet It does not involve the body at all.

The Holy Spirit instructs the mind very directly to drop ego thinking and belief. As you listen to the Holy Spirit you will find that taxes and bills get paid as long as you believe in them. The body is fed as long as you believe in it. Obligations and duties get met as long as you believe in them. Nothing is ripped away, yet everything is retranslated until the belief in specifics is dissolved forever.

This is why I have asked you to question everything you believe. Only false belief seems to limit your awareness. Truth is Abstract, and when the fear of Truth has gone, all pain and striving is over. Nothing is simpler than Being as God created One Self. Give your mind permission to BE Still and Know, and It is already accomplished. Give your mind permission to drop the pursuit, and you discover what has always and forever been so. The wheel of time was made to distract from the Still Center. Let go into this Center and peace is obvious.

Trust in the Holy Spirit will continue to grow. No one can accept forgiveness without trust. Trust is the basis on which miracles are founded. Trust is the way to open the mind and release false concepts and idols. Future planning can be laid aside, for Present Trust directs the way. Confidence and surety come with trust, and this is how you become aware that you are truly a miracle worker. Time is in your hands, so to speak, as you trust the Holy Spirit. Aligned with the Holy Spirit you no longer have an enemy to "overcome." For the Light has come!

I offer you this idea from *A Course In Miracles*. Let your mind be open to the release it brings right Now:

Trust would settle every problem Now. Be still, and be blessed in this Moment (T-26.VIII.2).

I love You forever and ever!!! David

GETTING TO THE BOTTOM OF BELIEF

Hi David,

I have a resurging question.

If I believe that I am the only one, that there is no one out there, it's all a movie screen, then why do I believe in being helpful to the characters in the script??? Who is there to be awakened? Why do some figures seem to have awakened when others seem not to have? How can some of the mind be asleep and some of the mind be awake? When I lay the body aside and the dream is ended... what about the other dream figures? I think you know what I am getting at. There is something here I haven't resolved, can't explain. Whenever you have time...

Love

Beloved One,

Thanks for your devotion to Awakening. Being helpful is being tuned in to the Spirit, and this helpfulness is in a Purpose of mind that offers only benefit. Your happy, joyful, peaceful, free-flowing state of mind is the gift, for it is our beatitude. This state of mind comes from being in Purpose and thus not taking anything personally. In the joy of the Living Moment there is no concern or worry for any of the characters of the script, for one has stepped back and is identified with mind – not body.

There is only one mind to be Awakened, and one mind Awake sees all the characters as the same. No character is ahead or behind, and no character is awake or asleep. All of the characters were constructs or symbols of the wish to have private thoughts and private minds. Awakening sees the impossibility of such an attempt, for one mind is unified and

cannot be divided and alone and separate. The happy dream brings an end to dreaming, because forgiveness is a dream of non-judgment. Then, as the Mind remembers It is Creation, Self, the illusion of dreaming is over and never was. When the body is laid aside in Atonement the cosmos is laid aside as well. Eternity remains as God creates, and there is no time in what is Forever Spirit.

Love always, David

IS IT EVER RIGHT TO GIVE UP
ON A RELATIONSHIP?

David,

This is a difficult question to ask. Is it ever right to give up on a relationship? Is it always the ego that is seeking for love and not finding it? I seem to see some couples that seem to have "loving" relationships, and yet, this eludes me, although I have been in the same relationship for over 35 years. I have struggled so often with the feeling that I am flogging a dead horse. Yet, because I have studied the Course for several years, I am deeply aware that the Son of God (my partner), always deserves my love, and honor.

When I get depressed about my relationship, I remind myself not to focus on what I want, but to refocus on how much I can give to the relationship – knowing that giving is receiving. Occasionally, there is a glimmer of light, but for the most part, it's cloudy. I don't want to give up on this person, or relationship – but it sure doesn't feel good. Your loving insight is greatly appreciated.

Namaste.

Beloved One,

Thanks for writing. In ACIM Christ teaches that the one right use of judgment is "how do you feel?"(T-4.IV.8.4) Yes, it is always the ego that is seeking for love and not finding it. And yes the Son of God always deserves our love and honor, for Christ is our Self. You have written: "When I get depressed about my relationship, I remind myself not to focus on what I want, but to refocus on how much I can give to the relationship – knowing that giving is receiving." Focus on the state of mind that you truly want; peace, and

see that your peace of mind is the gift you give. It is true that giving is receiving, for Christ extends peace and experiences the peace that is extended. Just remember that gifts are not made through bodies if they be truly given. Your beatitude of peace is the gift, and if you seem to be depressed it is because you are attempting to deprive yourself of giving/receiving the gift.

As a metaphor for Awakening in ACIM Jesus describes three seeming "levels" of teaching. These are stepping stones to learning that giving and receiving are one, for in Truth there are no levels of Love and this is a Course in Teaching Only Love:

"The teachers of God have no set teaching level. Each teaching-learning situation involves a different relationship at the beginning, although the ultimate goal is always the same; to make of the relationship a holy relationship, in which both can look upon the Son of God as sinless. There is no one from whom a teacher of God cannot learn, so there is no one whom he cannot teach. However, from a practical point of view he cannot meet everyone, nor can everyone find him. Therefore, the plan includes very specific contacts to be made for each teacher of God. There are no accidents in salvation. Those who are to meet will meet, because together they have the potential for a holy relationship. They are ready for each other.

The simplest level of teaching appears to be quite superficial. It consists of what seem to be very casual encounters; a "chance" meeting of two apparent strangers in an elevator, a child who is not looking where he is going running into an adult "by chance," two students "happening" to walk home together. These are not chance encounters. Each of them has the potential for becoming a teaching-learning situation. Perhaps the seeming strangers in the elevator will smile to one another, perhaps the adult will not scold the child for bumping into him; perhaps the students will become friends. Even at the level of the most casual encounter, it is possible for two people to lose sight of separate interests, if only for a moment. That moment will be enough. Salvation has come.

It is difficult to understand that levels of teaching the universal course is a concept as meaningless in reality as is time. The illusion of one permits the illusion of the other. In time, the teacher of God seems to begin to change his mind about the world with a single decision, and then learns more and more about the new direction as he teaches it. We have covered the illusion of time already, but the illusion of levels of teaching seems to be something different. Perhaps the best way to demonstrate that these levels cannot exist is simply to say that any level of the teaching-learning situation is part of God's plan for Atonement, and His plan can have no levels, being a reflection of His Will. Salvation is always ready and always there. God's teachers work at different levels, but the result is always the same.

Each teaching-learning situation is maximal in the sense that each person involved will learn the most that he can from the other person at that time. In this sense, and in this sense only, we can speak of levels of teaching. Using the term in this way, the second level of teaching is a more sustained relationship, in which, for a time, two people enter into a fairly intense teaching-learning situation and then appear to separate. As with the first level, these meetings are not accidental, nor is what appears to be the end of the relationship a real end. Again, each has learned the most he can at the time. Yet all who meet will someday meet again, for it is the destiny of all relationships to become holy. God is not mistaken in His Son.

The third level of teaching occurs in relationships which, once they are formed, are lifelong. These are teaching-learning situations in which each person is given a chosen learning partner who presents him with unlimited opportunities for learning. These relationships are generally few, because their existence implies that those involved have reached a stage simultaneously in which the teaching-learning balance is actually perfect. This does not mean that they necessarily recognize this; in fact, they generally do not. They may even be quite hostile to each other for some time, and perhaps for life. Yet should they decide to learn it, the perfect lesson is before them and can be learned. And if they decide to learn that lesson, they become the saviors of the teachers who falter and may even seem to fail. No teacher of God can fail to find the Help he needs." (M-3)

Your relationship with your partner is similar to most inter-personal, "couple" relationships and has been "... a more sustained relationship, in which, for a time, two people enter into a fairly intense teaching-learning situation and then appear to separate. As with the first level, these meetings are not accidental, nor is what appears to be the end of the relationship a real end. Again, each has learned the most he can at the time. Yet all who meet will someday meet again, for it is the destiny of all relationships to become holy. God is not mistaken in His Son." Very few "couple" relationships are third level teaching-learning situations "...because their existence implies that those involved have reached a stage simultaneously in which the teaching-learning balance is actually perfect." In third level teaching-learning situations there is always an inner experience of rapid spiritual growth or ego undoing. If you are experiencing sustained depression or a feeling of sustained stagnation in your relationship this is a Call to go within and listen carefully to the instructions of the Holy Spirit. The Holy Spirit needs happy learners and this requires the willingness to be flexible, and to trust and follow the prompts that are given to you. The illusion of depression comes from a sense of being deprived of something that you want and do not have. Remember that you are deprived of nothing except by your own decision, and be willing to allow the Holy Spirit to decide for God for you by aligning with the Holy Spirit.

Let the Holy Spirit Guide you with all seeming decisions, including the "to stay or to go decisions" involving relation-ships, jobs, locations, etc. You will seem to go through many changes as you Awaken, yet these changes are as temporary as is the forgiveness to which they lead. An experience will come that will end all doubting, and this experience touches the Changelessness of Spirit. Be willing to follow all the prompts of the Holy Spirit, and you will know you have by the light-heartedness, peace, and joy you feel within. This is the one right use of judgment and this discernment will lead you into the forgiven world and on to waking from the dream of separation entirely.

We are joined in this Awakening, and Joy and Happiness are inevitable for God's Will is for Perfect Happiness. It is impossible that God's Love remain unrecognized.

I love You forever and ever! David

GOD IS A PURE IDEA, AS IS CHRIST

Hi David,

I live in Australia. I continue to read from your awakening site with great interest, often it is so helpful and much appreciated. I notice that you don't seem to judge the ego, or at least the ego takes a back seat in your writings. Other sites emphasize it all differently. In a recent post, this point was made: If you believe that you know what Love is, and that you can of yourself forgive, or you have something that others do not have and you can give it to them (like love) you are believing that you are God. As long as you think that the world is real and that the body is alive, you believe that you are God. It would seem to me that we cannot go past this false idea of God because we cannot see without the ego.

When I first read the Course, God completely disappeared. I found myself saying there is no God. So as long as we are here we cannot know God. So do we see God as completely made up? The Course does say that even God is an idea. The ancient Gnostics used to be of the opinion that when one has transcended then one sees that you are THAT. To my way of thinking, THAT is our very essence. We become God. "Love is what you are." First we go through various stages till we grasp THAT. But we are always THAT (when the ego is out of the way). According to the above post, one is just being arrogant to think this way? Like a no win situation. The dog chasing its own tail.

Bless you for all your encouragement.

Beloved One,

I hope to visit Australia early next year or for a "Way of the Heart" conference near the end of August. It would be a Joy to meet you.

Forgiveness clears the way for Remembrance of God, so that is always the focus. Until the mind releases the error of ego, the fear of a make-believe "god" is buried deep in the unconscious mind. In this respect it takes forgiveness or release of the entire ego belief system before the Memory of God's Love can return fully into awareness.

God is a Pure Idea as is Christ. When the mind is emptied of false concepts and beliefs, the Pure Idea remains – Eternal and Perfect. "I am as God created Me" is another way of saying Love is What You are.

I am grateful that the web site has been helpful for you. Thanks for writing and I hope to see you soon.

Love always, David

FLOWING IN GRATITUDE

Dearest Davidji,

Gratefulness flows from this one towards your answers of the Holy Spirit. So much is made by the ego only to be undone again! It has reached levels of great humor and laughter is inevitable when one sees the futility of all those so called beliefs. One is beginning to become so aware of the greatness of God as myself and how this truth had never left myself!!! What to say of the "shelling" of this dust-like body that is not in any case. It is such a beauteous experience to be in alignment with Him who has never begun, continued or will never end. The Peace is almost unbearable if one may say so and the smokescreen of one's false ego just evaporates into nothingness...
lololololololol

One has been "doing" the lessons of the ACIM for the last 34 days. ACIM says that salvation is available in an instant... One attended the gathering at Plano, Texas. At that time one felt that salvation was already here with myself. Moments of awakening seemed like they would never go away. Here one returns to Dubai and finds that same salvation waxing and waning. The power of the "insight" does not fade but that ability to BE that ONE again seems somewhat tested from time to time. Every lesson uplifts one a little bit more and at times one feels one is literally flying... Is enlightenment like this? Up one day and slightly less the next? Underneath it all one feels a Peace hard to describe. It is with a fair amount of vigilance on one's mind of thought and ego that one returns to what I always have been, then the beauty of the Light shines again. Flip-flopping is what one awakened one called it...Why flip-flopping?

In love and Oneness with Him who is forever the Only truth.

Beloved One,

Thanks for sharing your heart! In our joining of Purpose the seeming flip-flopping ceases. This is the final lesson: The Truth is true and only the Truth is true. Truth is beyond a shred or scrap of doubt. What was the seeming flip-flopping, but doubt of Identity. Certainty takes the place of flip-flopping as surely as Love is Real. First one shall seem to unplug the ego, and then it seems as if the ego never was. I rejoice with You as the Spirit Now! Nothing can change Eternal Love. Glory to the One Who Creates in Perfect Love Eternally!

Love, David

GRATITUDE 2

Hello David,

Firstly, I would like to thank you so much for your love and devotion. You have been such an inspiration for me and many others. Your work, as well as Kathy's and Resta's, is greatly appreciated. It is such a blessing to have the online tools that you guys provide, as they always serve to deepen my understanding and bring God's Love into awareness.

I have been a student of the Course for about sixteen months now, and It has completely changed my life. It seems to have been a long and difficult road to get here but all that begins to fade and not matter as my mind is healed.

The Holy Spirit has used my transformation as a witness to His healing power and we have a small group now, which is so wonderful. It is the greatest thing, to see someone heal and experience the joy with them. I am at times filled with Love so intensely I weep tears of joy. God loves us so much!

I have been in correspondence with Kathy, and we are setting up a gathering here in Lafayette, LA in February. I am looking forward to meeting and sharing with you all.

Thanks again for everything.

Peace and Love Beloved One,

Thanks for your expression of love and gratitude. I rejoice in coming together with you and your group. Yes, the tears of joy flow so easily in such intense Love. Thank You God for your Gift of Eternal Life.

Blessings abound, David

GRATITUDE 3

Dear Loving David,

I have truly been moved and spiritually charged by the messages
you have been so thoughtful and generous to share by email.
Your responses are uniquely insightful and imbued with visions
virtually devoid of thoughts of the world allowing separation of
the heedless corporal world to the purposeful spiritual world of
eternal love and acceptance shining and radiating infectiously in
our spiritual essence into our conscious minds and expressions,
truly a miracle.

Loving Eternally All Things Of His Will.

Beloved One of God,

**Thanks for the gratitude you so eloquently express! It is a
Great Joy to serve the Will of the One.**

Forever grateful and in deep appreciation, David

FORGIVING FEELINGS OF BETRAYAL

David,

I feel betrayed by God... As strange as that is to say, if I'm being completely honest, that is how I feel. I am new to your site and I truly believe there is a reason our paths crossed. I'm 32 and I was raised in a Baptist church. I bought into what I was taught about God and Christ.

I believed that Jesus was raised from the dead and I believed that I was forgiven for all of my sins. I asked God to come into my life and to direct my path. For doing so, I expected to have peace of mind and happiness.

The older I get and the more disenchanted I become with my own life and the hope or possibility of me finding happiness and peace of mind, I feel as though I made a bad "deal." I feel as though I have been betrayed. Even though I have tried to be the best Christian I can be, God hasn't rewarded. Worst yet, it doesn't even feel as though God is there. I can't begin to tell you how awfully lonely that feels.

I have a counselor that I see regularly and we have discussed this in some depth. He tells me that my current view of God will only lead to more anger and resentment for me and that I need to change the paradigm in which I view God and faith. I agree with this completely but my problem is that I don't feel as though I can trust or put faith in God anymore.

I do believe that all the emptiness, loneliness, anger and resentment I feel could be resolved if only I could resolve this crisis of faith that I am experiencing. I'm reading this and I keep thinking what right do I have to feel betrayed by God. I know that I have been blessed and that there are those who are much less fortunate than I. Intellectually, I know this but in my heart, I feel so hurt and I just don't know what to do or where to begin. I would sincerely appreciate any insight you could provide me.

Thank you for your time.

Dear Beloved One,

Thanks for sharing what is on your heart. You are so precious and deserve to feel the Love that is buried beneath the hurt. Love is our inheritance or birthright. The ego (Satan in Christian terms) is a false identification, a mistaken identity, and the Purpose of our work with the Holy Spirit is to realize that the real Self is not the ego and remains forever the Perfect, Innocent Child of God in Spirit. The ego's feelings of betrayal run very, very deep as do the feelings of abandonment, loneliness, hurt, anger, emptiness and loss. The world was made by error so that God would NOT be discovered. It is indeed a profound step to ask God to come into one's life and direct one's path, yet as profound as this step is, it is only the beginning. The entire cosmos was made from the belief that it is possible to be separate from God or "fall" from Grace. Forgiveness is the undoing or release of the original error and all the errors that seemed to follow.

Jesus was raised from the dead to demonstrate that sin or error has no power. You have received the reminder of our Sinlessness and Perfect Innocence, the Holy Spirit, and now you are Called upon to release every spot of error to the Light of the Holy Spirit within your heart. Satan was the error that it was possible to leave God, and feelings of betrayal and resentment and anger arise from this unconscious error. Your counselor is offering a helpful suggestion by saying that you need to change the paradigm in which you view God and faith, for such is forgiveness. God is Perfect Love and Christ is a Perfect Creation.

What needs to be forgiven is the belief that God had anything to do with the time-space cosmos of duality and multiplicity, of sickness, pain, suffering, and death. What God creates as Eternal Spirit remains Eternal Spirit, and that which seems fleeting and temporal and transitory will fade and disappear.

The disenchantment and disillusionment you feel can be viewed in two ways. The ego would blame the feelings onto its "version" of God, an anthropomorphic view of a "god" of human concepts and traits who is "capable" of betrayal and abandonment. The Holy Spirit ever gently reminds that God is Spirit and Identity in God is Spirit. The Holy Spirit lovingly offers forgiveness as a replacement or Correction for dreams of anger and of pain. The mind is very powerful and the issue is never really an issue of faith or lack of faith – for what you put your faith in is the central decision. And every decision you make is a conclusion based on everything you believe, regardless if you are fully aware of what you believe. Satan is an unreal belief and while the mind invests in this belief, then "sin" or error appears to have reality and existence. Who You are in Truth is far beyond the "need" for forgiveness, yet the illusion of false identity must be forgiven or released that True Identity may be remembered.

Be happy and glad that you are beginning to see that there is no hope of peace or happiness in the appearances and forms of this world. Happiness and peace of mind are real and are found within as Christ teaches: "The Kingdom of Heaven is within." We are embarking together on what seems to be a journey within, and I assure you that happiness and peace of mind are inevitable and certain. I speak from the Perspective and the experience that this is the Truth right now. What is true for the One must be totally inclusive, for the Spirit God creates includes everything and therefore there is nothing apart from this Spirit.

As you continue to explore the web site and the audio and video materials it will become apparent that forgiveness applies to that which is false. That which is forever True (Spirit) is far beyond the need for forgiveness. God does not forgive, for God has never condemned, and yet there must have been an illusion of condemnation before forgiveness was necessary. The world is in need of forgiveness as long as you believe in its reality, for a world apart from God could never be.

Awakening to Truth is the dawning of the realization that it is impossible to leave the Mind of God. Such is Salvation or Enlightenment. I am joined with you in the Great Awakening. We cannot fail to remember Identity in God for illusions cannot veil the Truth. Please feel free to call or write or visit or meet anytime.

We shall rejoice together in God's Love, and in this experience of complete rapture there is only Joy! God knows Spirit as One and there can be no "body" that is "more" or "less" fortunate in the Perspective of the Holy Spirit. Let Us give thanks to God for creating Spirit as One forever. Amen.

I Love You forever and ever, David

HELP WITH LESSON 25

David,

Lesson 25 says that all goals are of the ego and asks me to relinquish them. Does this mean that I should not have any goals in my life? Should I then not even plan my day? How am I to survive in the business world where everything is goals and quotas?

Thank you.

Hello Beloved One,

ACIM gives the goal of forgiveness to replace the ego's goals of form outcomes that maintain the belief in separation from God. The Holy Spirit works with the mind, whatever and wherever it believes itself to be, and helps loosen the self-concept that the ego made to take the place of Christ.

I held a gathering many years ago in which the following Q & A dialogue took place:

Question: I have to go back to work today and do some computer work and some other things before tomorrow morning. I'd rather stay right here. You talk about intuition and Spirit leading you. Now how do I do that?

David: The Holy Spirit starts from where and what the mind believes it is. Suppose you believe you're a woman who has a particular job, and tonight that looks like having to do work at a computer. Let's suppose that this scenario is all just a motion picture of a belief system that you have, and that this is simply the way that you perceive yourself at this moment. The Holy Spirit doesn't try to yank this web of beliefs apart. The Holy Spirit will use those things that you believe in, to help you realize that you are much more than

the self-concepts in which you believe. This discussion, for example, is bringing witness to your mind's desire to wake up and remember your reality as the Son of God. All one has to have is the willingness, and the Holy Spirit will undo the false self-concepts and replace them with forgiveness. Start with this prayer: "Abide with me, Holy Spirit. Guide me in what to say and do and where to go." If you welcome and trust Him, you will experience immediate results.

Question: I'm having some trouble with the description of duality and that it's our perception that's the problem. I work in a business where I have to see things exactly as they are happening, not as I might like them to happen. So, the problem for me is in understanding how to get to that place that you're talking about.

David: It certainly seems that when one has identified one's self, for example, as an employee in a business, that there are "external" constraints and restrictions to abide by. For example, let's say one is identified as a manager. A manager is accountable to a boss, and a manager monitors and evaluates employees, directs them, conducts performance reviews and so forth. What one must do is look closely and go deeper into the belief system that is producing the faulty perception, that is producing the scenario I have just described. One must be willing to examine what one's priorities are, what is most important in one's life. Is peace of mind one's only priority?

I've had to take a good look at everything I believed, turn inward for strength and support, and realize with certainty that the Holy Spirit is my only "Boss" and forgiveness my only function. One may say, "How practical is that? What do you do when you have two bosses, if you have the Holy Spirit and your employer telling you two different things?" Again, the Holy Spirit meets the mind where it believes it is. He works with the mind, helping it to exchange accepted self-concepts for the more expansive self-concepts that approach true forgiveness.

As you lay aside judgment and change your mind about the world, what happens on the screen of the world will be a symbolic representation of that mind shift and of your perception of relationships. So really we're back to just saying, "Okay, Holy Spirit, work with me right now where I believe I am and help me loosen my mind from these false beliefs. Help me let go of the ego and my perception will be healed." Trust in the Holy Spirit for everything and He will take care of you in ways you can't even envision.

Let the Holy Spirit Guide you in all things and everything will work out for the best. The inner journey goes very deep, but the Holy Spirit Guides surely and there are many free resources available for the asking. I am joined with you in the Awakening. You are dearly loved.

Blessings of Peace, David

How Did You Turn Your Ego Off?

Hi David.

I wanted to say God bless you for all your love that you give.
My friend in Denver who has emailed you a lot is helping
me along my journey with a course in miracles. My problem
since I was even like 2 or 3 years old has been fear and always
thinking the worst. I wish I could just turn off my ego fear but
it has always been my downfall. I know I have to look within
and read more and meditate more. How did you turn your
ego off? Is it just constantly being aware and rejecting it at
all times. I worry so much it drives me crazy. God bless you
and thanks again for being such a wonderful spirit. We would
love to meet you sometime.

You have inspired us both so much.

Beloved One,

**Thanks for your question and for writing what is on your
heart. One does not turn the ego off, one unplugs it by
withdrawing faith in it. First you begin by paying attention to thoughts and feelings and perceptions. The chatter
and emotional roller coaster ride and distorted, unstable
perceptions attest to an insane ego belief system that dic-
tates these swings. The ego must be exposed and brought
to Light before the swings will give way to a consistent,
stabilized perception. Until faith is withdrawn from the
ego the mind will seem to swing between darkness and
Light. You made the ego by believing in it and can dispel
it by withdrawing all belief from it. Without the power
the mind seems to give it the ego will seem to cease to be.
Right Now Christ is Present. The ego was an illusion of
past/future, but the Light has come and in this Light the
error has vanished.**

Be willing to move inward and question all assumptions. Fear is an assumption and thus dissolves in the presence of Light. Protect no belief from the healing Light of the Holy Spirit and you will see that there is nothing to cling to. Yield and merge with the Will of God, for it is our Will as well. Miracles come from trust in God, and as this trust increases fear disappears. Your willingness will seem to open into readiness, and your readiness will seem to open into mastery. All glory to God and thanks to the Holy Spirit for Guiding past the illusion of fear to the forgiven world and on to the Memory of God.

Love, David

Chapter 4

WHAT IS THE MEANING OF "IDEAS LEAVE NOT THEIR SOURCE?"

Beloved Brother David,

In the workbook, Lesson 167, it states, "Ideas leave not their source." I have heard you and other students of the course quote this short sentence, but I do not understand the meaning of this statement, and I respectfully request your clarification.

In kindness and love.

Beloved One,

Thanks for writing. In Heaven this idea means Christ remains in the Mind of God and can never really "leave." With regard to this world the idea means that there are no problems apart from the mind because ideas leave not the mind which seemed to think them. Everything that seems to be "manifested in the world" are really thoughts and concepts, and thoughts and concepts never leave the mind that thought them. The ego's attempt at projecting thoughts to a seeming "outside cosmos" is delusional because everything is Mind and there is therefore nothing "else" at all. This is also why all seeming illness is mental illness and has nothing to do with bodily symptoms. Salvation or Enlightenment is therefore nothing more than escape from false concepts that have no reality or existence. This brings an end to the illusory idea that there can be an "inner" AND "outer," for mind is one in forgiveness and Mind is One in Reality.

Love, David

Is it Helpful to have a Guru?

Dear David,

Is it helpful to have a guru in your life, especially when you have dark night of the soul to go through? I have read that we all need some kind of help to undo all that we have learned. That's where Intercessory prayer comes in or a Guru with preferably a lineage that shows they have done this sort of work through the generation of their family. It all has to do with the energy of this individual and the group they travel with in spirit.

I study ACIM and find that I have grown tremendously in combination with all the other spiritual books and work I have been doing. However, I see now that even my guru has some unlearning to do. The course teaches us never put anyone on a platform and I see now. It has taken me a year and another dark night to see that I have put aside me knowing that there was another way to handle my illness. It was due to this guru that I postponed pursuing this. I believe the lesson maybe that we all have the energy within us and when my guru speaks like any other in life I must discern the info and go within for the final answer. Whenever I push away that urge I find obstacles in my path. So I'm confused, I see a major change in me with this guru but at the same time I find the advice can conflict with my most inner beliefs. I thought I must listen. This is the lesson: Listen to the REAL SOURCE – the one WITHIN.

Please help me to see what else I may be missing

Beloved One,

Thanks for your heartfelt and sincere e-mail. Role models such as gurus, teachers or guides are very helpful stepping stones as the ego is undone. They can be inspirational and very supportive witnesses to the mind's desire to wake up. They can offer very helpful and practical advice, teachings, and examples. Yet accepting the Atonement (Correction)

is THE sole responsibility and this is a decision of mind that transcends the concept of personhood. Persons do not become enlightened, for the mind that believes itself to be a person is asleep and dreaming of exile from the Oneness of Spirit. While the deceived mind believes in linear time Awakening will seem to occur in stages. During the seeming "process" of Awakening symbols are used by the Holy Spirit as stepping stones that reflect "higher" or "more expansive" states of consciousness. A guru can be a symbol of the potential for Enlightenment, yet the experience of Enlightenment is impersonal, unconditional, and abstract. The final "dark night" is always the temptation to retain a sense of individuality, privacy, autonomy, and uniqueness. All perceived darkness reflects the belief in private minds with private thoughts. Mind is one in forgiveness and One in Truth.

It is wonderful that you are seeing that the lesson of discernment always rests with the perceiver. Use your feelings as a barometer in this discernment, for how you feel is the one right use of judgment until it is apparent that any judgment is entirely impossible. Follow the Joy! Follow the Bliss! As you look within and make no attempt to protect or defend the ego, you will experience the Love the ego was made to hide. Love simply Is, and when the obstacles to the awareness of Love's presence have been removed only Love remains.

When you think of the concept of guru think of this:
Gee YoU aRe YoU

This is the gentle reminder: "I am as God created me." (W-162) This is the Power of Now. This is the simplicity of being. Truth is simple. The ego was the illusion of confusion and complexity.

In Love & Oneness, David

IS SEX EVER AN ACT OF LOVE?

Hello David!

I am writing to you from Miramar Argentina. I have been wondering what your view about having sex is? Sometimes I think that in a way that is a part of our ego, because we could think that that is our ego trying to make our minds think only about what the body might need. But I have talked it over with friends and we've come to the conclusion that depending on the situation or the person that you are with it is also an act of love, if you are doing it with the person you love. Acts of love are many, miracles I would call them. So what does A Course In Miracles say about it? What is your view?

Love always.

Hello Beloved One,

Thanks for writing! Sex in a loving relationship dedicated to the Holy Spirit and Guided by the Holy Spirit is (in this sense) an act of affection and can continue to be so until the mind has become so unified in Purpose that there are no cravings or desires for form of any kind. When this desirelessness happens there is truly the miracle of Atonement and Christ is fulfilled in the Divine Love of knowing God in Spirit. The miracle of Atonement transcends or dissolves the attraction to guilt in the sleeping mind.

Sex solely for the purpose of pleasure and sensual gratification is an ego motivation, attempting to reinforce the "reality" of the body, and this always involves the illusion of guilt. In ACIM Christ speaks about the attraction to guilt (pain & pleasure) and this involves the attraction to the body and world – so as one deepens in Awakening the desires for anything of this world evaporates or fades away – and Joy radiates from within! All seeming needs or lacks are gone in Divine Love. Let the Spirit within Guide you in all things moment by moment.

Love & Blessings! David

JESUS, CHRIST,
GOD AND THE LORD'S PRAYER

David,

Are "Jesus" and "Christ" synonymous? If so isn't that redundant? Is Christness exclusive? What is Christ? Can we be Christ? Is Sonship exclusive to Jesus? Are we to worship Jesus? Is there an ultimate God, as in the one Jesus referred to as "Father" in English translations. Why does Jesus teach his disciples "The Lord's Prayer" in which Jesus is not prayed to? Is there any separation between God and us?

What is the scoop!!!!!

Beloved One,

Thanks for your questions. Christ is a Perfect Divine Idea and Jesus is the name of one who demonstrates or represents or symbolizes this Divine Idea. The Name of Jesus stands for a Love that is not of this world, for Love is Eternal and the cosmos is temporary. Jesus Christ is therefore a symbol and the Love the Name represents is the Spirit that is One with God. True Identity is the Christ.

The Sonship is synonymous with Christ and Jesus was the name of one who recognized the face of Christ in everyone and Awakened from the dream of the world. Jesus is a demonstration of the Love that is the Sonship. Jesus points to God Who is deserving of Awe, and God is worshipped as the Spirit of God's Love is shared or extended. The attitude in which one treats one's brothers and sisters and everything is the attitude one has with the Creator, for these attitudes are one. The One God might be referred to as the Creator and is the One referred to in the Bible by Jesus as "Father." This term can correctly be interpreted as our Spirit Parent, for God is neither male nor female.

The "Lord's Prayer" was taught as a model of prayer for generations beginning at the time of Jesus, though God knows the prayer of the heart before a word is ever spoken. Prayer is a medium of communication between the Creator and the Creation in which Answers and Divine Experiences come forth. To pray to Jesus is to pray to the Holy Spirit, for Jesus and the Holy Spirit are synonymous in function. They lead to Atonement or complete forgiveness and the happy dream that brings a close to all dreaming. In the Lord's prayer Jesus is praying with everyone to the Creator.

Even the Bible statement "I and the Father are one" has two parts in that Christ is the Creation and God the Creator. Creation and Creator are One Spirit and share the same Will for Perfect Happiness. There is no separation between God and God's Creation. Forgiveness of illusion or error is its release, and this leads to Awakening or remembering God's Eternal Love.

Blessings be upon You Holy One, David

KARMA REVISITED

Hi David,

I cannot let go of this question of karma. Everywhere you turn someone has something different to say of it. Poonja said, "I don't believe in karma." Another said, "even after awakening there is still karma of the body." What is going on? Does anyone really know what it is? Does karma equal cause/effect? If so, then this whole nightmare, this hallucination, belief in separation, that's the karma. But even then, when there is a so called 'awakening' the body's still hanging out. It doesn't disappear. And sometimes it still hurts or sneezes, or eats or sleeps. I really do not understand.

Do you?

Beloved One,

Thanks for looking deeply at this universal law of mind. It has been written: "As you sow, so shall you reap," "Giving and receiving are the same," "What goes around comes around," "Cause and effect are one and there is no gap." This one universal law of mind has seemed to bring harm and destruction to the mind which seems to sleep and dream of a separate world of unreality. Yet this one universal law is the key to forgiveness. If you realize that you always choose your state of mind and that what you choose you choose for the whole universe, the belief in victimization has been undone. Misuse of a Divine law seems to result in miscreation until the realization dawns that in Truth it is IMPOSSIBLE to misuse or miscreate. What God creates is Spirit and Spirit creates only Spirit. If you follow this divine logic then there is the experience of Enlightenment: Truth is true. Love is real. Nothing real can be threatened. Nothing unreal exists.

The body was a symbol of a separate self that could never be. The enlightened mind sees the tapestry of the forgiven world in which no object or specific exists "in and of itself." Illusions are one, and thus the illusion of a "body" and the illusion of a "time-space cosmos" are the same illusion. In forgiveness there is nothing that is "still hanging out," for perception has integrated and is whole. There is nothing outside the Mind and the cosmos reflects the Light of Heaven. Only a blessing remains and distortion has gone.

Since karma is a universal law, the only meaningful question is "What is it for?" What will you use karma for: to demonstrate that healing is accomplished or to maintain the wish to be separate? The first use is inevitable and the second use is impossible. It is best to accept the inevitable and release the attempt to make the impossible possible. Such is simplicity, for Enlightenment is simple.

In Heaven God and Christ, Cause and Effect are One. From the Holy Spirit's Perspective mind is unified and cannot be broken apart. The law of karma can therefore release or imprison the mind based upon the mind's use of this universal law of mind. Purpose is the only choice. Which purpose would you have it serve: love or fear? When you align with the Holy Spirit your Answer is Love. And the experience which comes from aligning with God is so obvious that you will never doubt again.

Peace be with you always, David

WHAT IS THE FEAR?

David,

Could you say something about my neck being in spasm for a week, during a time when many beliefs are being examined and seen as false. There are also other physical oddities. I would like to hear what comes to you regarding letting go.

I'm sitting at my computer, physically tired, feeling sad, peaceful, and a twinge of anxiety. So, you are here to guide me through. I also feel a little cold, which seems to go with fear sometimes. What is the fear? Holding back the sadness. What is the sadness? That there is no perfect scenario, no perfect person, place or thing I can turn to. The only thing is right now. I notice that going home sometimes is scary; I think that I'll get home and there'll be nothing I want to do, that all the distraction (for the ego) and the meaning (talking with you, practicing presence, following intuition) is "out there."

Why have I made home feel like a prison sometimes? It represents shoulds. But if I give up all my shoulds: I should recycle, I should pay bills, I should take care of the yard, I should buy groceries, I should clean things, I should water plants inside, I should call the pest control, I should wash clothes, there will be no me. That's sad. No me to love and be loved, no me to take care of things, no me to be kind, honest, smart, or original, no me to give advice, no me to be a good mom or a good friend, no me to even follow intuition and feel "good" about it. No me. There's a knowing that walking through that letting-go-process allows the peace that surpasses understanding... AND a more powerful knowing that I'm afraid to let it all go.

So, I continue, ball by ball, to empty the basket (Eckhart reference.) The sadness comes from seeing that I have built my own prison and refuse to leave it, as it is familiar... As I confess my illusions, their hold on me lessens.

Thank you for listening. I am peace now.

Beloved One,

Thanks for writing out the stream of thoughts and for your willingness to see beyond them. Whether the discomfort seems physical or mental, the Solution rests in acceptance. You are not responsible for the error, only for accepting the Correction. Do not project the error to the past or future and you will see you are free of it Now. You are afraid of the Present Moment Correction, believing it requires of you everything that seems to be familiar to the little "self." Yet forgiveness asks for nothing. It rests on the idea that the Truth is true Now and Forever, and sees that all concepts are false. The miracle shows that nothing Real can be taken away or lost. Be glad that there is no perfect scenario, no perfect person, place or thing to turn to. Right Now is Always Everything and forgiveness is never circumstance dependent. Forgiveness is the concept of now, and as this concept dissolves and melts there shines Eternity in awareness.

Align with God and it will seem the dream is happy from this new Perspective. Be happy paying bills, happy taking care of the yard, happy buying groceries, happy cleaning things, happy watering plants inside, happy from the Purpose that is far beyond the "doings" of a body. When at rest in mind everything and everyone is still. It dawns that things shared in Purpose are effortless and easy. Personal effort is not required in beholding God's glory. Accept divine ease, and there is nothing to be concerned about. You cannot lose Who You are, for God created You as Perfect and You remain so.

The Correction clearly demonstrates that Love is all there Is. Do you want the "problem" or the Answer? Love is never difficult. Love is natural to a mind that trusts. Spirit is trustworthy. You cannot mess up Who You are, so there is nothing left to doubt. Now is the only obvious choice for accepting this simple Fact. Blessings shower upon You Holy One.

Love, David

Releasing the False Belief

Dear David,

I take care of the "seeming" body of the one who gave this "seeming" body birth. In so doing, am I promoting the belief in myself and in my brother in the illusion of sickness? The body lies there, not communicating, not moving, eating, etc. It is seemingly healthy, yet the mind does not make it function. Sometimes my brother looks at me. Sometimes my brother seems to be my mother. Sometimes, but seldom, I have talked to her, sometimes to my brother, reminding him of who he is; that is, when I am moved by the Spirit to do so. In those times the eyes lock on mine and seem to be connecting and resonating or absorbing, or something. If I speak on any other premise, such as saying what I am going to do (like move or bathe the body) or if I ask a question, the eyes shut real tight and avoid looking at me.

I play Resta's songs next to the bed during the day. At any rate, I seem to have a brother who has chosen to cease moving or communicating, yet has not yet chosen to lay the body down. At least, in my understanding, this is what seems to be happening. I seem to have no choice in this matter. At least I have not heard any guidance from the Holy Spirit, or perhaps I am not willing to hear if it is saying to put the body in an institution. I am sure if Holy Spirit was saying to do that, He would make a way and give me peace about it.

Not until I met Resta did I begin understanding my brother is my teacher, and I seem to still be learning through my experiences with this brother. Perhaps my brother is waiting for me to know that we are one. Sometimes my brother looks at me expectantly, seeming to be searching. Or perhaps my knowing will help my brother to know.

Have you any answers for me?

Beloved One,

Thanks for your e-mail. Everything you think and say and do teaches all the universe what you desire, believe, think, feel, and perceive about yourself. Recently I wrote what Christ shares in ACIM about the holy encounter: "As you see him you will see yourself; as you treat him you will treat yourself; as you think of him you will think of yourself." (T-8.III.4) Everyone is our brother/sister in Christ and is due immense gratitude because they mirror what is still held in mind and believed to be true and needs to be released. Your state of mind and your perception are always your choice.

Only you decide what you desire, believe, think, feel, and perceive. There are no "external factors" in a decision of mind for there is literally nothing "outside" of mind. The question is not really "what to do?" but instead "what do you want to see?", for what you want to see is what you believe you are. Every question is a question of identity, and while you believe in a make-believe self-concept that God did not create, your choices are limited. Your ability of choice is limited to either aligning with and choosing the ego's personal perspective or aligning with and choosing the Holy Spirit's Perspective. This is your range of choice and you have no other. Decide to accept Atonement and the concept of choice vanishes entirely, for in Heaven or Reality or pure Oneness there is nothing to choose between.

Decide for the miracle and you feel the peace of a mind that is whole and a glimpse of wholeness. Decide for the ego and you feel stuck in a frustration and conflict of trying to be something that you are not. You wrote that you see a body that is not functioning and needs to be cared for. This is a mirror perception of what the ego mind believes is true. When you allow the Holy Spirit to share ideas through you, you perceive one who whose eyes "...seem to be connecting and resonating or absorbing..." What does this tell you? It tells you that you have a function the Holy Spirit would have you fulfill by allowing Him to speak and smile through you.

You have a Purpose to share true ideas, thus strengthening them in your awareness. What you teach is what you learn, and thinking is teaching. You are teaching all the time based on what you desire, believe, think, feel, and perceive about yourself.

Your function will carry you far beyond a bedside, far beyond Alabama, far beyond the time-space cosmos, for your function will carry you to the Gate of Heaven, the Atonement. You have a Light to shine. Do not hide this Light under a table. You have a love for the Bible and can speak for God using the inspired words and verses of the Bible.

The opportunities are many and they are waiting only on your answering God's Calling for you. You will be a teacher of God and will seem to speak to many in the years to come. And through this function you will find the experience of the Answer you have requested, for Who You Are is the Answer that everyone who walks this world seeks. Christ is the Answer! Love is the Answer! You will be given specific instructions and direction from the Holy Spirit once you are willing to hear them. There are many answers you have received but have not heard. The Holy Spirit is holding these answers you seek for you until you are ready to hear them. They all reside within your heart and await the readiness of mind to be heard.

I close with a quote from the Bible: "That which is born of the flesh is flesh. That which is born of the Spirit is Spirit." Is your brother/mother flesh or Spirit? Remember, as you see your brother/mother you will see yourself. And remember that the Way God created You is Reality: Perfect, Eternal, Innocent, Loving, Spirit which has no opposite :)

Love always, David

LOVE IS BEYOND
THE BELIEF IN ATTACHMENT

Dear David,

Forgiving illusions means forgiving what a body does. If a body cheats or lies, hurts our body, or takes something away by deception, it is still not deception because we are attached to that something and this can include our own body which is an illusion. It is our attachment or belief in illusions of things or body that can make us judge others or feel hurt or angry or say it was unjust. If we recognize that only spirit exists and it is all powerful and cannot be hurt then nothing that happens here matters. And we see everyone and everything from the point of wholeness. Even the 'deceitful' thing that happened is probably to teach us a lesson not to value anything including the body of this world. Thus we see sinlessness in all persons, things, and events.

If something happens that feels disturbing (fearful) we just have to think that it will not have any effect on our living. This is really hard. We are afraid of losing our friends, family, our living conditions, etc. I just have an understanding of these principles but have no firm conviction. Then we also have to develop present trust that the Holy Spirit will provide for all our needs as long as they are necessary.

But first we have to experience miracles and that we are Spirit and for conviction and inner knowing to come. Is it not? Otherwise, it will be just based on theory. How do we get these miracle and Spirit experiences? In spite of doing ACIM, I have not had any such experience to speak of. At least this is my understanding of Christ's vision. Would you provide us with some insight into this? As always your valuable vision is tremendously appreciated.

Thank you.

Beloved One,

Thanks for sharing what is in your heart and for your sincere opening to the Spirit within. You have written what you are just beginning to grasp:

"It is our attachment or belief in illusions of things or bodies that can make us judge others or feel hurt or angry or say it was unjust. If we recognize that only Spirit exists and it is all powerful and cannot be hurt then nothing that happens here matters. And we see everyone and everything from the point of wholeness. Even the 'deceitful' thing that happened is probably to teach us a lesson not to value anything, including bodies of this world."

Miracles bring conviction for they demonstrate what you have just written – the valuelessness of the body and world and the value of the Spirit which is unchanging. Miracles are experiences that dissolve belief and collapse time. If you are willing to question what you seem to believe, and apply the words you have spoken to everything in your awareness, the experience of inner peace will be evident. If you seem to be "...afraid of losing our friends, family, our living conditions, etc." then there is an identity attachment to these things which is blocking the experience of the miracle.

The miracle costs nothing and offers a glimpse of Everything. There is no sacrifice in knowing God's Will and our Will is one with God's Will. Nothing real is lost or given up in serving God because the temporary never had any value whatsoever. All that is of value is Eternal and even a glimpse of this fact brings immediate peace of mind. If you apply the principles of miracles and make no exceptions you will experience what I am writing about. Words can but point to the experience of Love that is truly far beyond words.

Who is family to Christ? Who is friend to Christ? What are living conditions to Christ? Everyone and everything, for mind is one. Everyone and everything is included in healed perception, the forgiven world. Christ sees no body and no thing as special or unique or distinct or different. Divine Love looks upon ItSelf and sees only Perfection. Love makes no comparisons for there are not "two" of anything to compare. Welcome to the Oneness which sees that there is nothing apart from Mind, which experiences the family of Spirit. Christ is Friend to all and the beatitude of friendliness is universal and all-encompassing – it cannot be limited to a person or group of persons. The Living Condition of Spirit is Joy and anything that seems to be of form can at most be a reflection of the Joy of the mind that hears only one Voice. In Purpose the mind is unified and specifics and details fade in importance, for Abstraction is the natural condition of the mind.

It is important to practice what you are beginning to grasp. Share these ideas as the Holy Spirit directs and this sharing will strengthen them in your awareness. You cannot give away what you do not have. By sharing these ideas you become aware that you have them and you will see that you are them. You are a perfect Idea in the Mind of God and nothing is ever "lost" by giving your Self away. Share Love and know that You are Love. Share Love and see that there is nothing "outside" this all-encompassing Love. You are the Light of the world, for God creates only Light and God is our Creator.

Blessings of Love always, David

MIND WATCHING
WITH THE HOLY SPIRIT

Dear David,

I'm writing this mainly to help me retain the value of our phone conversation by reviewing what I perceive as most important for me to remember.

First and foremost is the idea of impersonalizing and generalizing anything that arises in my consciousness that is contrary to God's nature, anything inharmonious, seeing it as a manifestation of the primal error of believing it's possible to separate from God. This I would do with the help of The Holy Spirit by saying in effect, "Holy Spirit, help me to see through to the Truth that this illusory appearance is a lie about."

Connected to the above idea is the idea of "making no exceptions," or endeavoring to be vigilant enough to ask the Holy Spirit to help me hold everything up to the light of Truth, everything without exception, and to ask for the Holy Spirit's Guidance in every situation without exception.

And the idea that the ego's inclination to conceal an erroneous appearance so that it won't be dissolved by the above described process, is prevented or at least reduced by surrendering or accepting fully whatever experience is being served up at the moment with full attention of the experience in the Now moment.

And finally, your idea of "simplicity" such that what's written above is as "complex" as the process need be.

Also, I felt much more of your being my "shepherd," so to speak, always available ("call anytime") and always reliable (YOU yourself make no exceptions to the Truth). Connected with this is your encouragement to write to you about how

I'm doing, which is another way to hold whatever's going on up to the light of Truth, and which also opens up another powerful avenue through which Guidance can get my attention and get its point across through the content of your replies, whenever a reply is called for.

In closing, thank you again, David, for having "worked on yourself" so as to have become a being of such exceptional "Purity" where I feel such assurance that your comments will always be, without exception, "Purely Divine" and feel so relaxed and comfortable.

I will write you much more frequently from this point forward, in the realization that just by having the current content of my consciousness being known by someone whose consciousness is a few octaves higher in Divine Purity than my own, helps greatly to loosen the more encrusted, or more hidden, erroneous beliefs, as well as giving you the opportunity to give direct Guidance in a reply whenever your own Guidance indicates that that's called for.

Thank you, David. With much Love.

Beloved One,

Thanks for your openness and willingness to hide nothing from the healing Light of the Holy Spirit. When darkness is brought to Light, when illusion is brought to Truth, darkness/illusion disappears. The ego's seeming "existence" was "maintained" through deception and concealment – like a complex hall of mirrors – and the cosmos was made as a distractive device to guard against exposing and dissolving the original lie (the belief that separation from God is possible) and accepting the Atonement (Correction). From the belief in separation and one with it came the belief in private minds with private thoughts. This belief induced the illusion of guilt and therefore it is this belief which must be exposed as false.

Enlightenment or Salvation is simply seeing the false as false, and this distinction is made with the Holy Spirit's Perspective. Such is discernment. Your willingness to watch your mind with the Holy Spirit, yielding to Love and turning over all judgments and comparisons, opens the mind to the Present Moment. Thanks for sharing your experience of mind watching for the benefit of the mind which is engaged in the "practice" – Practicing the Presence of Now.

Love, David

NOT GOING ANYWHERE

Dear David,

The Course says: "Why would I choose to stay an instant more where I do not belong, when God Himself has given me His Voice to call me home." (Lesson 202) "...I am His Son, Not slave to time, unbound by laws which rule the world of sick illusions..." (Lesson 204)

My question is this: You have written that desire for salvation is enough. We need do nothing and in fact everything is done for us by the Holy Spirit and we cannot add anything to it. Also we need not come to the Holy Instant already healed of our fears. It is meant to heal us. If these statements are true why am I still here in spite of many years of practice and the strongest desire possible? Why, is it so hard for me to have atonement and what am I doing wrong? Thanks for your help!

Sincerely.

Beloved One of God,

Thanks for your sincere question and devotion to Awakening. You have "done" nothing wrong in the Great Awakening to purity of Heart. All "doings" and "behaviors" and "perceptions" seemed to spring from a heart that desired God AND desired idols. Single desire might be called desirelessness, and this is the State of Creation. This is the meaning of "Let thine eye be single" and points to spiritual Vision or Light. Vision does not involve the body or perception, yet this Vision is veiled from awareness as long as desire is split. The entire time-space cosmos is nothing but a reflection of split desire. As you attempt to meditate and sink into Perfect Stillness you will notice the ego's resistance arise. This is the resistance to the "do nothing" experience of "Be still and know that I am God." It will seem difficult to do nothing while you still believe in the ego, in personality, in linear time-space.

The ego was false belief. The ego was the belief that Creation could be broken into meaningless bits and parts. The "I" that seems to be "here" after "many years of practice" is a self-concept that has no Reality and has been dissolved by the Holy Spirit. The past is gone. This self-concept included "you" and "you're family and friends" and the entire cosmos that seemed to surround the personality self. Now mind is opening to the acceptance of this solution, this dissolving, this undoing in the Present Moment or Holy Instant. Look directly and calmly with the Holy Spirit at everything you are not, and happily Who You are remains forever and ever untouched. Let go of all transitory thoughts of past and future, and Who remains is the Present Self God creates forever perfect.

It is hard to resist accepting Atonement, for forgiveness is the most natural experience one can have with regard to this world. What God creates, Spirit, is forever Natural. Anything which seems to cover over the Natural is not natural and can thus be easily forgiven or released.

Look at what is believed with persistent determination to see beyond belief with the spiritual Vision of Christ. By desiring only God the remembrance of God comes back into full awareness. False desires will go for they have no foundation, no reality, no source. Only desire Truth, and then watch and observe that all "seeming" decisions are already made. Effortless observance or witnessing is ours as the dreamer of the dream. Nothing can touch the dreamer who remains aware that the cosmos was but a dream.

All glory to the One for creating Spirit perfect. Gratitude to the Holy Spirit for beholding the dream as false from a Perspective of happiness and peace. We are joined in this holy Perspective! Love & Blessings shower upon the Living One.

Love always, David

NOTHING HAPPENING
AND NOT SEEING

Hello David,

I appear to be in a situation that is calling for forgiveness, but despite all of the reading of ACIM and your web site and your ACIM group, and all of the meditating and lesson applications, nothing seems to bring peace to this situation. I am very much aware of two sides to my mind. One side wants very much to forgive, but another part of me wants very much to 'punish' the perceived wrongdoer (i.e. project the anger). My means of punishment is attempting to blatantly 'ignore' and make the other person aware in a roundabout way that I am pissed off with them. Intellectually, I can see that ultimately this other person has nothing to do with my problem, but the ego wants to make this person know that they have hurt me (make sin real).

I cannot seem to just forgive (i.e., do nothing: merely look, wait and judge not) because when I do I get a strong feeling of loss, that any opportunity (i.e., special relationship which I feel cannot have come from anyone else) that might have existed with this person has gone forever, and that scares the s*#! out of me.

Saying things like "these thoughts about 'person x' do not mean anything," and saying "God is the love in which I forgive 'person x'" or "...myself" over and over just hasn't worked (because they are just words to me because the experience that they are pointing towards just isn't there), and I'm really becoming aware that deep down, I DONT WANT TO FORGIVE THIS PERSON, I WANT TO HATE THEM. I feel like I am in an impossible situation where I cannot see any outcome that will satisfy me COMPLETELY and that's the scariest thing of all, because I can see only despair. Yet despite my desire for special relationship I still want enlightenment, I want to understand completely, to see the truth.

I am tired of meditating, I am tired of repeating the lessons because they don't work: NOTHING HAPPENS. I'm still left with problems, I am still left with complete non-understanding, and I am no closer to enlightenment.

Decisions used to be difficult for me, but now they have become so much more difficult. The procrastination is almost unbearable. I get caught between ego goals, and cannot give over decisions to the Holy Spirit because I can't trust that it's actually the Holy Spirit directing me.

I'm just not SEEING the one decision I need to make, I'm not SEEING the 'heaven option', not seeing that choosing for form and the world is actually a choice for nothing, and no amount of reading, studying or meditating is helping in that seeing.

That's all I feel like writing at the moment. I trust that you will make sense of the above. I know that you've answered all of this sort of stuff before, but it just isn't getting through and I needed to write.

Beloved One,

Thanks for writing. I am grateful that you could write out everything that is going on in your mind. And I know it is helpful to get in touch with the full extent of the ego's hatred before one can let it go. It is very necessary to allow these feelings to arise in awareness before you will be willing to let the hatred go forever. The hatred still seems specific and still has a target in the world, yet as the deepening continues it will seem more and more nonspecific. The ego's anger is actually at God for not granting reality to the time-space cosmos, but this hatred of God is kept out of awareness. The belief in competition with God mentioned in lesson #13 is usually not allowed into awareness, for it is too threatening to keep in awareness. So the ego uses the unreturned "love" of the special relationship to attempt to justify the anger until the deeper hatred at God and fear of God is exposed. But

in looking deeper the "original error" is uncovered and the ineffectiveness of the special relationship becomes acute in awareness.

Give your mind permission to let the seeming beast rear its head. You will go past these feelings and be free of them. Simply do not attempt to protect or project them, and they will dissolve.

I am joined with you in going through the darkness to the Light within. We cannot fail.

I love You always Beloved, David

CAN I HAVE A GATHERING?

Dear David,

How simple and joyful my life is when I think about how all the pain and suffering in the world isn't real. But it is hard sometimes with all that's been happening in my life. I'm sure this year has been hard for everyone. I've tried to solve everyone else's problems and at the same time avoiding and making my own problems worse. This year has been beyond stressful. I started 7th grade last year and it has been one of the hardest changes in my life with friends, teachers, and family. The work is very overwhelming. Both emotionally and physically hard times. I'm usually a straight A student but this year it all went down the drain. My family is also very stressed right now. My mother who introduced me to the Course of Miracles is the one I turn to when I start to give in to depression. And I help her when she needs it even though I try to help everyone and have even explained to some friends who wanted to know the truth.

Have you ever done of your gatherings in any towns in NV? My mother and I would like to invite you sometime. I have one question. Would it be for anyone, even people who had never read or heard of the Course of Miracles? I've been listening to Resta's songs and find them very touching. I was even thinking of holding a gathering of my own this summer and share some of the songs with people. I would love any advice or comforting words from you.

God Bless You.

Beloved Child of God,

Thanks for writing and for your dedication to Awakening to the Truth within. Trials can be used to strengthen your faith and call you deeper within. It becomes increasingly apparent that we cannot solve other people's problems and always

need to watch our own mind. This is truly our full-time job. I have received invitations to several cities in your area so maybe we could have a gathering at your home when we are Guided to come to the Southwest. It is a great idea to have a gathering of your own and share inspiring music.

The Love will shine through you to people who have never heard of the Course as you let the Holy Spirit direct. When people see your Light they may then be curious and ask to know more about what you think. There is never anyone to convince since peace is an internal matter. Your life will be profound and inspirational. Do not be concerned about the grades, and always remember that you have the Light within when you are tempted to be depressed. You have entered the 7th grade but your wisdom is beyond the learning of subjects and information. You are the Light of the world and everyone is blessed by every step you take in unlearning the ego. I am with you every step of the way.

Blessings of Love, David

OPENING TO DIVINE PROVIDENCE

Dear David,

I have been so blessed to have received much from you these past few months. Being a student of ACIM, I am aware of how giving your life to God is a serious undertaking. I seem now to be torn between really trusting God and wanting the trust of the world. I have debt that I owe and cannot pay back right now. It greatly distresses me because I want to make things right with the people I owe and I just don't have the money. I become scared that I will never get it paid back and will always wander under this burden of being a failure financially. I am really trying to be under no laws but Gods. And I am really aware of my true inheritance. I just want to be free. As I write this, I am getting a clear message that I am free; I am just going through a period of sorting out – and it's pretty uncomfortable.

My irresponsibility in the finance department is one of shame and distress sometimes because my family was so successful. I do have great need of seeing this differently. I used to base all my hopes and dreams and visions of "success" in dollar signs. That is changing, but not completely. I still must see this as a way to measure my worth. My worth was established by God and I need to remember that. I have a long, long way to go spiritually. I am still looking at the two worlds. How do I resolve this? Can you help? I'm sorry to be a bother. I really need understanding.

Love

Dear Beloved One of God,

It is an honor to hear from you. Rest assured that a request from you is never a bother and that you never need to feel sorry for anything or apologize for anything. Our worth is truly established by God and nothing that is said or made or done or undone can change Whom God created perfect.

Together we are questioning the ego belief system so that the Holy Spirit may reveal the Truth of our Identity in God. Your questions are sincere and there are beliefs about debt and responsibility that need to be uncovered and released. The fear of future consequences i.e., "I become scared that I will never get it paid back" is only a cover or distraction away from the fear of the Present Moment. The Present Moment is the Point of Intimacy with Christ and God, and nothing is so fearful to the ego as the Moment in which it is undone and dissolved away forever. This is another way of describing the resistance to extended and deep meditation.

It is helpful to be reminded that financial debt and financial irresponsibility are only projections of the debt of ego belief and the denial of accepting the Atonement/Correction for the error (our SOLE responsibility). You are not responsible for the error, yet you will need to see the error exactly as it is (in mind) in order to accept the Correction, which is our responsibility. The cosmos was the ego's attempt at "seeing" the error in form, thereby concealing itself (the error) from being uncovered as merely a belief in the mind. The ego was made by false belief and is undone by withdrawing all belief from it. The ego is anger and guilt and fear and uses these emotions along with denial and projection to maintain these unreal emotions which keep the Light beneath it concealed from awareness. The Light is buried deep within and we must go through the darkness of false belief to reach the Light of Truth (the Kingdom of Heaven within).

The ego (or Satan in Christian terms) is the belief that debt is possible. It is the belief that something is lacking, something is owed, and something needs to be paid back. Debt implies a repayment for something that was borrowed or taken away, yet in God there is only completion and Eternal Giving and nothing CAN BE borrowed or taken away. The belief in debt is the same as the belief in scarcity, and this belief has nothing at all to do with God – Who is All-Loving and All-Knowing and All-Powerful. The belief in debt needs only to be raised to awareness and forgiven or released, for debt has no reality on which to stand. The Holy Spirit is sorting out the true from the false in your mind, and you can rest assured that the ego and all its concepts of debt and economics and abundance and scarcity are false. Our Inheritance is Spirit and the Holy Spirit leads directly to the remembrance of Eternal Spirit and Divine Love.

As you perceive yourself in awareness "you" have needs, and if you are willing to be a miracle-worker you will increasingly recognize those "needs" as being handled through our Higher Purpose. All needs have already been dissolved in the Atonement/Correction, yet while the mind seems to invest in the ego belief system it will experience the illusion of debt. Miracles show that the mind is sustained by the Source of Love, God, and thus the mind is willing to relinquish all false concepts of sustenance. The mind asleep (everyone who seems to walk this world and believes in its reality) believes in the "laws" of economics, scarcity, supply & demand, and reciprocity. Miracles undo these false "laws" by demonstrating that the mind is not bound by them. It is impossible to serve two masters and it is therefore impossible to serve the ego AND the Holy Spirit because they teach opposite lessons. The ego teaches imprisonment/guilt/fear and the Holy Spirit teaches Freedom/Innocence/Joy. Financial freedom is therefore a contradiction in terms, for freedom is of and for the mind and cannot be found in specific forms such as money and possessions.

The Holy Spirit is Guiding you surely. You can trust this because it is true. The ego is being undone in your awareness and "it" seems to feel "pretty uncomfortable," "shameful," and "distressing," because "it" seems to be vanishing. It is always helpful to be reminded that You are not the ego, Christ is not the ego, and Spirit is forever of God and is our True Identity in God. As you become more confident in allowing miracles to be performed through you it will dawn in awareness that Mind is One and there is nothing apart from Mind.

I am with you every "step" of the way, for we share the same Self. Salvation from illusion is certain because no illusion can stand in the Light of Truth. We walk together on the Self same road and must recognize our Oneness to remember God. There is literally nothing "else," for Love is All.

Blessings of Love shower upon You Holy One of God.

Love, David

Chapter 5

PHYSICAL PAIN, ENLIGHTENMENT, KILLING AND VEGETARIANISM

Dear David,

I have so much enjoyed the news from your gatherings in Argentina. I could feel the joy all the way out in Los Angeles! It is a beautiful, warm day here, and birds are chirping outside the window of my little studio apartment. My two hairy children (cats!) are content and lazy. As for me, I am letting God creep into my day, and He/We feel wonderful!

I have a couple questions that I could not find answers to in the archives. They are rather peculiar, but the ego keeps bringing them to me for some reason. If you have the time, I would love to hear your thoughts on these questions!

1) When one is enlightened, does one still experience physical pain as unpleasant? Does one experience pain or displeasure about ANYTHING? Another aspect of this question is: Once you awaken completely, are you still vulnerable to falling back into ways of the ego, or is it ALL gone for good?

2) Do you think the Holy Spirit would EVER guide one to harm or take the life of another being? (ex: meat eating, killing ants in your kitchen, using violent force to stop a murderer, etc.). And, by the way, do you eat meat, and if so would you personally take an animal's life?

Once again, thank you so much for your guidance (and patience with our silly ego questions)!

Dear Beloved One,

Thanks for asking the questions that come to your mind, even if they seem "rather peculiar" to you. In Enlightenment all perceived pain has vanished, for what but wrong-mindedness seemed to produce the misperception called pain. Pain was the illusion that Christ could leave a Loving Creator's Mind. "If pain is real there is no God. If God is real there is no pain." (W-190.3) The latter is true because God has no opposite. Enlightenment entails no pain or displeasure about ANY-THING, for Enlightenment is pure, constant Happiness, Peace, Freedom, and Joy. Being constant, Enlightenment knows not of change. The illusion of vulnerability and fluctuating emotions has gone as well. There is no ego to fall "back into." Spirit abides ...in gentle Love. All pain is over Now and nothing remains but a blessing of Stillness.

The Holy Spirit is the reminder that Life is Eternal. The Present Moment is the gateway to Eternity. The world of images was a world of illusion. Images are therefore neutral to the Holy Spirit. They were "neutralized" the instant they seemed to arise. What does this mean in relation to your second question: You cannot kill what has never lived, and in the Holy Spirit's Perspective of forgiveness harm is impossible. Bodies were never born and never die because the world of images is the past. It is impossible to find beginnings and endings in a script that is already written and over long ago. There is no life in images. This is the meaning of "Hold no graven images before the Lord Thy God." All images were made to obscure the Truth from awareness, and they can only be forgiven as one illusion. If illusions could be divided up into living and dead, organic and inorganic, animate and inanimate, Enlightenment would be impossible.

For what is Enlightenment but Pure Oneness, far beyond the possibility of division of any kind. The split mind was the illusion. Seek not to project the split mind to forms and call some forms alive and some forms dead. God knows not form. The split mind seemed to be the "killer" illusion, yet the Holy Spirit reminds the sleeping mind that what is whole and unified can never BE split. In Heaven, Mind is One Spirit, and even with regard to this world, forgiveness reflects this Oneness. The forgiven world recognizes the Unity of the healed mind and sees that there is nothing "outside" of this single mind which dreams softly a happy, gentle dream. The goal of ACIM is to dream softly of a sinless world. This goal is more than possible, it is inevitable!

As for my seeming diet, "eat what is served" is the Guidance I was given from the Holy Spirit many years ago. Join with your brother and let no concept come between the Love you share. This Guidance has not changed. "Dinner" is always a backdrop for sharing the Joy of the Living Moment. What the world calls "breathing" and "eating" and "drinking" and "sleeping" are really all the same in the Enlightened State. The healed Perspective sees the sameness of all things because they all share the same Purpose: forgiveness. This Perspective is not "personal," for in unified perception nothing is personal. God is no respecter of persons.

I literally cannot "take" an animal's "life" because Life is Spirit and can only be extended or Given as God Gives. "Take" has no meaning in my mind and since animals have never "lived" it is impossible that they could "die." The belief expressed in the thought "personally take an animal's life" has many underlying assumptions that are false. In right-mindedness it is obvious that ideas are strengthened as they are given away or shared, and "taking" a "life" or anything at all has no meaning. All that I give is given to mySelf, and in giving there is no loss, no sacrifice, and nothing is ever taken away from wholeness and unity. The teacher of God does not want anything that cannot be given away. Such is the Joy of miracles! The thought seeds seem to be flung everywhere, yet there is never even a glance back to see where the seeds land. The seeds are never for an "other," and since giving and receiving are the same the mind receives the gifts it gives. This is truly the feast you seek for underneath the ego's questions.

The only question that need be asked is a question that is not really silly at all: Am I ready to know that God's Will and My Own are the Same? God's Will for me is for perfect happiness. And what but this Will is the Will of Christ? Happily, nothing can change Eternal Love. Thank You God! Blessings of Love abound!

Loving You Holy One, David

HOW SHOULD I PRACTICE THE WORKBOOK LESSONS?

Dear David,

As always thank you very much for giving your wisdom. I have a few questions that have been nagging me. I am not able to understand clearly how I should practice from Lesson 170 forward. Should I follow the recommendation given in Lesson 153? In some lessons it is written that we will experience something not of this world. In lesson 129 it says "...and in the silent darkness watch the lights that are not of this world light one by one until where one begins another ends loses all meaning as they blend in one. Today the lights of Heaven bend to you, to shine upon your eyelids as you rest beyond the world of darkness. Here is the light your eyes cannot behold. And yet your mind can see it plainly and can understand."

Firstly I did not quite understand this. Secondly I had no such experience. Other experiences are also described in other lessons which we are supposed to experience. I think I am doing the lessons diligently. But I have not had one such experience. Did you get those experiences described on the same day that you practiced? Is there something I need to do differently?

It is said that the script is already written. The time when the experience comes has also been decided. This means whatever has to happen, happens. If that is the case where is choice? This also means everything is working perfectly. Even the mistakes that we make are supposed to happen. But at the same time ACIM says that by practicing some lesson (I do not remember the lesson number), we can save a thousand years or more. If the script is written and the time is already set how can we save time? This is really extremely puzzling to me. And what is there for us to do than just wait for that time to come? Yet Lesson 169 says "...you have work to do to play your part." Elsewhere in the text it also says "You need do nothing." These seem like contradictions and I am totally confused and in dark about the meaning of these statements. Would you please enlighten us?

Thank you very much.

Beloved One,

Thanks for your sincere questions. The Workbook is designed as a tool to help Guide you to an experience that has been called transfer of training. In the Workbook are guided imagery exercises, meditations, visualizations, and very specific instructions to be adhered to as closely as possible. Some will seem to experience the lessons from a verbal predisposition, some from a visual imagery disposition, some from a silent predisposition, and some from a very emotionally sensitive disposition. None of this matters because the Holy Spirit meets the mind wherever and however it perceives itself.

The lesson to be grasped is always the lesson of non-judgment: "I do not know." Whenever judgments or comparisons arise they are suitable opportunities to remember the lesson of the day, release, and re-center on Purpose. The visual imagery used is always symbolic and intended to Guide the mind toward a transcendent experience. As best you can, do not attempt to judge anything which seems to occur, for this Workbook and Course and Manual is a curriculum in the relinquishment of all judgment.

"The script is written" means the cosmos is past. The choice is the miracle, to see the past as over and gone, instead of believing that the future is different from the past. The images are past, and this experience is pointed to in lesson #7, in which this new "time idea" is introduced. The deceived mind, asleep and dreaming, believes that it lives in the past. Yet Life is Eternal and the closest approximation to Eternity is Now. The Workbook lessons are designed to help release everything you think you think, and everything you think you see, to behold the Light beyond the veil – the Present – and See with the Vision of Christ. Miracles seem to prepare the way for Revelation, Pure Light, the Holy Instant, in which the Great Rays are experienced directly.

Apply each lesson with such overflowing passion, as if there is nothing else but Enlightenment to experience this very moment. Desire is the key, and this is the meaning of "I need do nothing." Doing is always a body thought. As you proceed you will find the lessons are but starting points to go beyond the words to the experience of Divine Silence.

All Glory to the Living God of Pure Light and Love. Amen.

David

PREGNANCY AND PARENTING

Hello David,

Welcome back from your trip to Argentina. It is wonderful to get your emails again. They always seem to come at the right "time." I have had several new developments in my "life" recently one being that I am expecting a baby. At this moment I am in my 7th month. As you can imagine this has been a very exciting and challenging time in my life on many levels. After reading your transcripts of the gatherings in Argentina I would definitely say that many of my unconscious belief systems are coming up to be unlearned. It has been painful, but joyful also. When the fears and pain come up I continually pray and ask for guidance from the spirit within.

I guess I would like your thoughts on the experience of motherhood/parenthood and how the Course sees it. And also how to continue to deepen my walk with spirit while also "raising" a child. Thank you. I look forward to your insights.

In love & peace.

Beloved One of God,

Thanks for sharing what is on your heart and for your willingness to use everything for Awakening. Everything that seems to happen in this world is truly just a backdrop to allow the ego's unconscious belief system to come up and be unlearned. Rest assured that all things work together for good and chance plays no part in salvation from illusions. While some spiritual traditions emphasize going off to a monastery or a convent or to the woods or mountains, the Course is a path that involves releasing judgments and grievances in the context of mind, including what appears in awareness as perceived interpersonal relationships.

Motherhood and parenthood are aspects of personhood, and this is the construct that one is freed from in Enlightenment. The Holy Spirit uses the symbols of the little make-believe "self" and gently Guides the mind into broadening vistas of consciousness. You are far more than a mother or parent, yet this backdrop of parenting will be a rich opportunity for the undoing of the authority problem. You will behold the forgiven world.

This world was the belief that it is possible to author a self different from the Christ Self God creates Eternally in Spirit. The simple word for this insane belief is pride. Pride is false authorship. God is the only True Parent or Author, the Creator of Reality. And so it can be said that "parenting" with relation to bodies and body thoughts is the opportunity for the undoing of pride. The path before you is filled with many, many seeming opportunities to release the belief in self-authorship and control, the belief that a body can be a separate self that can be a "separate, unique individual."

The body symbolizes the belief in private minds with private thoughts, which IS the ego. Yet given over to the Holy Spirit the path before you is a rapid undoing of every scrap of ego pride and control and resistance.

A child is a mirror of what you believe you are, as long as the belief in differences persists in awareness. A child is an ancient unconscious belief system coming up into awareness to be unlearned. To love as God Loves, unconditionally, the obstacles to the awareness of Love's Presence must be exposed and released. A child presents the opportunities to forgive every seeming grievance in the sleeping mind, so that Divine Love can be expressed without doubt or reservation or limit. This is a Moment of Gratitude and Joy, for Now can the lesson be learned that there is no concept to hide and no concept to protect from the healing Light of the Holy Spirit. Now can the mind be emptied of every opinion and judgment it sought to lay upon itself. For Innocence is real, and the Christ Child within is ever innocent of error.

Accept the Christ Child within by becoming willing to behold the Perfect One and completely unwilling to behold error of any kind. When you see that the Child abides in You and literally is You, the Spiritual Self, the need for time and lessons is no more.

May Blessings of Love shower upon You and Bless You, Holy One. I rejoice with You in this precious opportunity. I am with You every seeming step on the road to our Home, and because of the One Who goes with Us there is Great Joy! Angels hover over and keep watch, for the time of Awakening is nearer than a breath. There is a sparkle in the eyes of the one who knows of the many miracles that will be bestowed in this happy dream. There is a playfulness and lightness everywhere, for Christ has come to behold the Eternal Innocence that is the Heavenly Inheritance of everyone who seemed to go their way separate and alone. The illusion of separation cannot continue to seem to last, for the Light has come. Let our Light shine, and be the Beacon to light the way that once seemed dark and alone. Now the Christ Child can be no longer hidden from awareness. And we give thanks that this is so!

In overflowing Love, David

PARENTING AND SPIRITUALITY

Hello David,

We are so grateful for this opportunity. Please speak to us about parenting and spirituality...

Hello Beloved,

Yes... when things seem to come to us in this world, including children, they are just bringing to us an experience that we have asked for in a form that we believe is possible. So the Spirit has to use our belief system and bring us things that seem to satisfy our prayer. Some might call this manifesting.

The most important thing is the prayer of the heart. The deeper you go into spirituality, you see that you can only ask for an experience. And you see that the form never brings you the experience. The emotion is always coming from your own consciousness. As you get wiser and more mature, your asking changes; the request from a teenager can seem different than one from a wise master. The teenager might pray for a car or a boyfriend or a girlfriend, the wise master might say; I want peace of mind. So our asking changes as we go through life, until we fully see what the deepest prayer of our heart is; to know our true identity.

We need to let go of old ideas about teaching and learning since we are teaching and learning with everyone. We are really teaching with our thoughts, and what we always teach is something about our identity. The one lesson that we need to learn on earth is the lesson of Perfect equality, independent of the size of bodies. Really this one lesson is an experience of Oneness. Parents have an authority problem because they believe that they created the children and therefore have authority over them. When a child around two years old says things like "mine!" or "I will have it my way" it is a key opportunity to hear the call for love and a call to recognize the equality, that no one is a boss over anyone else.

Certainly infants and very young children seem to need a lot of care and attention, but this is just an opportunity to let the intuition come through in a way that is most appropriate. It seems like the parents are taking care of the child, but again it's an opportunity to see the Perfect equality. That's really what mother-child bondage is about. It's not really a bonding between the bodies. Jesus teaches us that minds are joined and bodies do not. It's more like a telepathic bonding in which you just relax and feel the connectedness. It's an opportunity to relax and enjoy every moment. It's a feeling of connection, the mother is not judging the baby, not thinking about the future or the past, not even thinking about a name, she is just in an experience of connection. To feel that connection is the goal of all our mind training by letting go of our judgments.

Everyone is a mirror of the thoughts in consciousness. Therefore the child is a mirror to the parent and the parent is a mirror to the child. And this is the reason why we never can blame our parents for how we feel, because our parents and our environment reflect the thoughts that we hold in consciousness. What you see comes from what you think. So parents are never to blame and children are never to blame. There is never a justified, good reason to point a finger at a parent or a child and say "it's your fault," because it's never anybody's fault. It's always the consciousness seeing a world and thinking the thoughts, and the world always reflects the thoughts. This is directly from the Bible: "As you sow so shall you reap." It's another way of saying "all that you give is all that you receive." It's always a perfect equation. That's why I'm saying be careful what you pray for, because you always get what you pray for. You can be sure that you are receiving what you are thinking. There are no exceptions to this.

So when a parent says "I'm having problems with my child," this could be reinterpreted as "I'm having problems in my consciousness." You could even say "my child is reflecting my problems in my consciousness" or "my child is reflecting my issues." Of course this applies the other way too. When a child has a problem the child can say "I have a problem in my consciousness."

More and more, the human race is evolving towards awakening. Every new generation of children that are born reflect the Divine Light of Love. Sometimes they call them Crystal or Indigo children, and they are just reflecting higher and higher states of consciousness. So this is really a benefit for the whole planet. Jimmy Twyman has done conferences on this. He went to Japan and met a very small boy who could bend spoons with his mind. And children have been known to have many psychic abilities which are very natural for the developed mind. These abilities are carried over from their previous spiritual development. So it's important to be open minded, which is what you are when you have let go of past learning.

We all have ideas about families, reflecting ideas that stem from memories of the past. Many of these memories are unconscious. Sometimes parents say they want to raise their children differently from how they were raised by their parents, but they are shocked when hearing themselves say the very same words that their parents said to them. Since the past repeats over and over we have to break out of the patterns of the past. Recently Eckart Tolle wrote the book *A New Earth,* and we might say that we're working on a new Perspective on the family. It is really a family of God; it's a new way of conceiving of families that has nothing to do with biological bondage.

We have to leave over the control to the Holy Spirit. Human beings can't be partially in control, just like you cannot be partially pregnant. As you begin to see the value of turning things over to the Holy Spirit you can start to include people around you in that. When you are guided to, you can sit down with your child in certain situations. For example if the child is sad for some reason, you can ask the Holy Spirit for help together with the child. Help the child with a change of mind about the situation. Really, if you change your mind the world changes with it. So another way is just to demonstrate that. We can teach the children what we would learn, since they are part of our practice and we are part of their practice.

Here are four main questions about parenting and spirituality:

- How do we talk to our children about spirituality?
- How do we talk to our children about the difficult things in life?
- How do we help our children develop to safe, happy and responsible individuals?
- What are children's spiritual needs?

We will now get into the answers of those questions as well as answers to some follow up questions. The first question resulted in the three guidelines from Spirit:

The first guideline: Don't talk about anything related to spirituality that you have not experienced yourself. That would only teach speculation. If you do not have a very clear, deep, direct experience of God, why would you try to explain it to your children? It will only lead to more questions and you might look like a fraud or a phony since your answers would not be genuine. It is a profound thing to be in prayer, in the experience of Spirit's guidance with what you say and do.

The second guideline: You have to speak what you're trying to convey in very simple terms because if it gets too complicated the children will just lose interest. Mean what you say and say what you mean. When you talk to children about spirituality they want it to be practical, they are not really interested in theories about God. Let's look at an example: Are you afraid of letting your child swim in a lake in the woods without supervision and without a life jacket? Why, if you teach that you don't believe in bodies and death and vulnerability? They want to talk about things that are related to their practical experience. So it's important to use lots of examples. You need to be very familiar and very sure about your ideas. A good parent uses a lot of examples because he/she is clear on the subject matter.

The third guideline: Address the child's area of curiosity. If the child never expresses any interest and curiosity about spirituality and God, then that is a sign to consider. It's not like teaching mathematics or science. The child has to be ready. And if the child is curious, then it's an opportunity for you to express your own curiosity in those areas. In many cases there is no invitation to explore these areas. So by talking to children about what they are interested in you show the children your care and attention. It's not in the words that you say – it's in your attitude and the state of mind that you express. This is where the teaching comes in. That's why Jesus taught about the be-attitudes in the Bible. It is teaching of a way of being, a state of being. We are not to correct our brothers and sisters and children, and a better way is to just wait for them to come and ask for help with their issues. So we should never try to correct our children in their ideas and views about spirituality. Every situation is always an opportunity to become clear for ourselves.

Question: How do we talk to our children about the difficult things in life?

David: It is good to talk about belief. There are many different beliefs, even around topics like death and murder. For an atheist and for a religious person, the view of death can be very different. Tell your child that no two people see the same world. To an interested child you can say that everyone that comes to earth operates upon a belief system. They organize their life by this belief system. If they ask you about conflict, like war, or conflict among their friends, you can tell them that there are so many beliefs and that these beliefs conflict per definition. If they then ask "why", it may be an opportunity to talk about error or ego, because the child is going to keep asking why. So tell them that as long as we believe in the ego there are going to be conflicts. We know that no two people see the same world, but there is a Love and Oneness that is beyond belief. The only one Helpful belief that exists is forgiveness. Forgiveness goes by many different names in different cultures. This is a good topic for discussion for the parent as well as the child, because both will teach and learn that subject for many years to come. Both will have many, many opportunities to forgive. If the child is curious, teach forgiveness! Tell the child about forgiveness. But the most important thing is always the demonstration of a state of mind.

Question: How do we talk with our children about belief systems?

David: Initially it will be better received and more applicable to talk about many belief systems, because the children see many people. And each person seems to operate on a different belief system. But the more you interact with children and the more the trust and the curiosity builds – they might look at you and say, "can't you make it even more simple?" Then you can tell them that though it looks like many there are really only two belief systems. One brings you Hope, Freedom, Peace, Love and Joy and the other brings you jealousy, hurt, guilt, fear and anger. If they ask you "why would anyone believe in hurt and fear" you can look at them and say "I'm working on the same question! That's why I'm here."

Question: How do we help our children develop into safe, happy and responsible individuals?

David: To the extent that you come to true safety, true happiness, and true responsibility, to that extent you can extend the gift that this experience is. We can't really do anything for anyone else that we haven't experienced. Our fears become reflected as their fears, and our guilt becomes reflected as their guilt. So it's always an inside job. Even when you're tempted to be worried and concerned about them it is always better to take it back to your mind and see "ok, I am the one feeling worried and concerned – it is something in my mind to release."

Question: Isn't it like telling the children, do as we do and not as we say?

David: Your relationship to the child is very much like Jesus' relationship to you. Jesus is the same as all of us; he is like an elder and wiser brother, (though we sometimes may seem to debate whether the parent is wiser than the child). But Jesus would say: Think like me, don't do like me. He doesn't ask you to put on a long robe, walk around and be crucified. He doesn't say "do like me," he says "think like me and do as you will." This means that the doing and the emotions flow from the thinking and that the emphasis is always on the thinking, not the doing. Apply that to your way of relating to children. If you are truly feeling peaceful and joyful and trusting, you can say to the child "think like me and do as you will." And if you are really happy, chances are they will want to follow you. And if you are very conflicted they will not want to follow you. They will look elsewhere for guidance.

Having children can be a great opportunity to practice intuition, because you cannot watch over the child constantly. You have to be intuitive and trusting. The priority is always to be at peace, and a means is to let go of the belief that you can control behavior. You can never control the world of form, and the child's behavior is a part of that. So the parent has never a direct control over the behavior of the child. It is actually impossible. You can control the direction of your thinking (ego or Holy Spirit) and that's the one thing you have control over.

In A *Course in Miracles,* Jesus tells us there are two thought systems, one of love and one of fear. And you can reach the highest potential by practicing listening to the Voice for Love and using the thought system of Love consistently. So in A Course in Miracles Jesus says: "You may believe that you are responsible for what you do but not for what you think, but you are responsible for what you think, and what you do comes from what you think."(T-2.VI.2) So instead of trying to control the behavior, which is an effect, just come back to the Mind, or the Consciousness which is the Cause, and make a change in your thinking. This doesn't seem to be easy. Many people try to behavior modify, they try to quit smoking, control their weight, not drink so much alcohol, etc. They have great difficulty trying to modify their behavior, but feel they would have even more difficulty trying to modify their thoughts. The only lasting change comes from changing the thoughts.

If you try to control the behavior but you still are upset in your mind, you still have a split in consciousness. If you try to act good but have anger underneath, your mind is split. Everything has to be in complete alignment. Beliefs, emotions, thoughts and perceptions have to be in alignment to have peace of mind. So with children it takes lots of practice. Parents say their own behavior is very important because of the belief that we learn from behavior; the idea of being a good role model. But children don't really learn from behavior, everything comes from thoughts. So therefore you don't have to try to act good because the child can often see past the act and know when the act is fake, and this is a good reminder to be authentic. If you tell your children to not fight and then fight with your husband, or wife, or partner, you need to change your thinking. You need to demonstrate a State of Peace.

Question: What are children's spiritual needs?

David: The only need anyone really has is to truly know Who we are. The ancient Greeks said "Know Thy Self." But you have to first meet the lower needs, like hunger, thirst or the need of warmth. You have to meet the seeming physical needs before you can go to the deeper needs of the Awakening soul. Mother Theresa knew this very well. Therefore she picked people off the streets to help them out. She didn't just go on the streets talking to the children about God, she took them in and cared for them. So for her and her sisters it was very much an act of service. She saw everyone literally as if they were Jesus. It was an example of "As you treat the least among you so will you treat Me."

As you become clearer you become more and more intuitive about what the true need is. Often children will express ego needs, in terms of toys or candy for example; wanting more and more. That's when you see that you have to be more intuitive. You don't want to get into confrontations, instead you are allowing through an experience of Love that is for both of you. This is the miracle. It blesses everyone equally. Sometimes parents try to treat all their children the same way. They try to give the children an equal amount of certain food or drinks or ice-cream. But it's impossible to work equality out in form. Instead, the focus is that we want to be equally loving and equally open to everyone. So the content of Love is important, and not the form of its expression. It is always a question about Self honesty.

With your child you can take every opportunity to teach Love, to teach what you would learn. It works in any situation. If you have fear of letting your child feel free, and move around unknown people, for example, you can take the opportunity to teach the child about the belief in privacy in this world or the idea of attack thoughts. Yes, just teach what you would learn! A very helpful tool is also to start to see everything as being just Love or a call for Love. Then you start to answer the call for Love wherever you see it. It might be your child coming in to your bedroom in the night, afraid after a nightmare, or a child hitting another child. Sometimes you may think that you are personally responsible for the child, for example if the child gets lost. But finally the idea of being personally responsible for anything has to go. No body can really be responsible for anybody. You are always only responsible for accepting the Holy Spirit's healing Correction within. Children and parents give each other lots of opportunities to learn the lesson of complete forgiveness. It can be the fast track to Awakening instead of being perceived as a burden.

Blessings and Love, David

THE FRUSTRATION OF
PRETENDING TO BE HUMAN

Dear David,

I am always glad to get the letters you have answered to others. I file them for reference and study. I have another question if you should be so kind to answer. In 1976 I had an experience that lasted over several months wherein nothing seemed real, and I was asking "what is real."

It seemed to begin when I read a book an acquaintance gave me, a story about a Guru Nanak, wherein he said something like, "Even though you carry around a cart load of books, unless you know Him, you have no knowledge." I believe he was talking to various religious groups indigenous to his homeland. Around that time, a voice within me seemed to tell me several things, and my life has never been the same.

The first message I heard was, "If you are busy pretending you are something you are not, you will never know who you really are." I kept asking what was real, looking around and saying, "Is this real, is this real?" And the voice within me would say no, that it was an illusion, here today, gone tomorrow, now you see it now you don't. Up to this point I had no spiritual knowledge except through protestant churches, Presbyterian, Baptist, Christian.

One day after work I was sitting on my bed. (I had come to look forward to rushing home from work, getting situated on my bed and getting quiet, as it was there it seemed, I found a presence of peace, as if a light would be around me and my questions would be answered. At that time, I thought the presence was in my bedroom.) On this particular occasion, after being told that this, then that, was not real, I asked vehemently, "Then, What Is Real?" The room seemed to fill with light. The light seemed to be coming from the inside of me. The moment was full of peace and a sense of absoluteness, and it said, "I am He and there is no other." Well, somewhere on the inside of me, that resonated. I called the entity Spirit.

For the next couple of months it seemed to be the only thing that seemed real to me, and I couldn't seem to keep from telling everyone, "We are One. There is no other," as it resounded on the inside of me, even though I couldn't seem to explain it beyond that. That particular occasion set me on a spiritual journey searching through all religions, trying to find that surety that I had experienced. The "spirit" continued talking to me throughout this journey. It was not until I began studying ACIM that I started getting the same message as that initial message, and it hearkened me back to that occurrence, which I had pretty much chalked up to my being Looney and desperate to feel special, so I had concocted it myself. Before that happened, I could not find my niche in this world, but since that happened, I have had absolutely no interest in anything except searching for what I called the "truth."

Nothing else seemed or seems to have purpose, and it is so hard for me to get out of the vicious circle of thinking I should get busy with this or that, dreading it, feeling guilty for my feelings, etc. I could make myself do the things I had to do, such as raising my family, keeping my home orderly and clean, but I have such a difficult time in wanting to do anything.

I told you about my shop before previously. The shop is just a refuge in which I can be alone to meditate, study, listen to ACIM tapes, music, etc. However, when I have an arrangement to create for someone, I put it off to the last minute, seemingly dreading it. Once I get started, I peacefully, neither enjoy it or otherwise. I just do it, as if I am not doing it, and I am always surprised that it turns out to be more wonderful than the customer dreamed, because, when I look at it, I seem to have no judgment of it at all. All I seem to know is that it is finished and I can do no more.

I found some fabric in my sewing box the other day, and thought to make my granddaughter a dress out of it. I purchased the pattern and notions, and now have no desire to do it, and am absolutely having to make myself do it. It seems to have no purpose. When I get like that, I seem to be paralyzed about everything, even studying the course and workbook. When I think of the things that are waiting for me to do, I cannot seem to let go of thinking I ought to do them, I get confused about which I should do first. When I let go of thinking about them at all, asking the Holy Spirit to give me unction, I find it hard to be at peace not doing until then. Then I just get tired, and seem to want to sleep. I know that "shoulds" and "ought to's," have echoed in my head all my life, but I haven't seemed to be able to extricate myself from them. All this truly does seem to be vanity, to serve no purpose. Everything I do just seems to serve this illusion, and I have wanted to escape it ever since that experience in 1976. Help! This is beyond explaining. What do I forgive to find release? How do I return to peace?

Beloved One,

Thanks for pouring out your stream of thoughts and for your willingness to forgive and Awaken. It is wonderful! You have heard the Voice for God reminding you of the illusory nature of the world. With *A Course In Miracles* you have a tool to train your mind to hear ONLY the Holy Spirit's Voice and release the ego's voice of doubt forever. In using and practicing the lessons of ACIM you will be forgiving the belief in separation, the belief in time-space, the belief in a linear sequence of separate events. You will experience many miracles which will collapse time and leave your mind at Peace. You will grasp and experience the Holy Spirit's Purpose, which is the replacement for the ego's "purpose" of death, guilt, fear, and separation.

You first glimpse the new Purpose of forgiveness, of seeing the illusory nature of the cosmos, yet until the ego's "purpose" is completely unlearned or undone you will seem to wander. It can seem during this wandering that the world will have no purpose at all. This is the approach to the point in mind in which you see that the roadways of the world lead nowhere. As the mind approaches this point everything will seem pointless, yet beyond the point of utter meaninglessness

is the Light of the Holy Spirit. As you join with this Light, the Light will shine through you and radiate to everything and everyone. The Holy Spirit shines through you, shining away every scrap of darkness, and this experience is one of effortless Ease. There is no struggle or conflict in being shone through. It is as though you are transparent, for there are no personal goals or agendas to intrude.

The Holy Spirit Guides surely. In every seeming situation the judgment of the Holy Spirit directs. This is judgment through you rather than by you, and under the Holy Spirit's judgment there is never any loss to anyone. In the Holy Spirit's Purpose there are never any commands or demands, only suggestions and instructions and reminders. You can seem to resist the Holy Spirit's Call, yet delay is always temporary and Atonement or Correction is inevitable. That is why this is a required course. Forgiveness is unavoidable, and though there seem to be many forms and pathways for coming to forgiveness, in content they are all the same. Forgiveness simply sees the false as false, and quietly rests in Peace.

The voice of "shoulds" and "ought to's" is the ego. These guilt-ridden expectations arise from a false sense of self, a self-concept that God did not create. This concept was make-believe, for it sought to replace the Self God created in Eternal Perfection. All frustration arises in consciousness from pretending to be human, and all human roles are constructs that perpetuate this pretense of identity. In the Present, free from the distortions of the past, You are free in Spirit as God created You. You have been inspired by Resta's music, now you can be inspired by Resta's release of the story of "mother." You have identified as daughter and mother and grandmother, and these roles have limited your awareness of the Christ. Christ has no limits, Being Eternal.

Forgiveness offers you an expansive self-concept in which everyone and everything is included, a Perspective that leads to Waking from the dream and remembering Christ and God. You will discover that Christ is Reality and not a concept at all. Make believe self-concepts need defense only because they are shaky, unstable, and unreal. Spirit is

always defenseless for in truth there is nothing real that can be threatened and nothing unreal that exists. Herein lies the Peace of God. Resta recently forwarded this e-mail to me that she had sent to her "biological son":

Resta: "I woke this morning realizing that I must have a "heart to heart" communication with you. My life now is all about being in purpose: forgiving the illusion of the world and remembering my true identity – with you and everyone – as Christ: pure abstraction, spirit, light, love. My task at the moment is the complete undoing of personhood, the construct of body, personality, private mind and set of masks made up to replace my true Self. And that includes all the roles I devised, such as "wife" and "mother." Last year as I was working through the separation from Bob, I received a song, "I Release You," and I share it with you now because it applies equally to my relationship with you:

"He who was enemy is more than friend when he is freed to take the holy role the Holy Spirit has assigned to him. Let him be savior unto you today. Such is his role in God your Father's plan." ACIM W-78.5

I RELEASE YOU (song lyrics)

You don't have to pretend to be someone you're not,
a puppet who moves on the strings of my thoughts.
The role I've assigned you has cheated us both
of the light and the glory that lives in the soul,
but patiently yields to each mask we put on
that proclaims we're not children of God.

I release you, my brother, to be who you are,
my savior, the Christ who abides in God's heart.
And I'll be there with you, for we're truly one,
beloved of the Father, His Son.
You don't have to be little, unloved and unknown,
clothed in a body that you call your own.
You're not a husband (son) and I'm not a wife (mother),
for mind has no gender and form has no life.

It's time to remember what we always knew,
that God has one Son, and not two.

Refrain
You are not a person and neither am I.
We forgot we were dreaming and living a lie.
Now Spirit is calling, My dear child, awake,
let God's sweet love heal you, correct your mistakes.
Be married to all, for the all is just One,
God's holy and blessed Christ Son.

*When you were about 8 years old you made me a Mother's Day
card that I found recently. On one side it said "To The Very Best
Mother" – and on the other side you wrote, "Mother is my brother."
We have come full circle, back to that recognition you had then. I
am your brother and only your brother. My "motherhood" is done.
I love you as a dear brother in Christ, as I love Bob, as I love
everyone. Everyone IS myself, and I exclude no one, make no one
special. That does not diminish your value but makes you infinitely
precious, to me and to God.*

*I bless you on your journey that has no distance, back to the home
we never left. I am always here for you when you want to connect
heart to heart. Dearest one, I love you forever and ever. Resta"*

**Forgiveness is giving up nothing to accept Everything. Mind
is unified, and peace and wholeness go together. You have
asked: "What do I forgive to find release? How do I return to
peace?" To forgive the belief in time-space is to say to God:
"Show me Eternity!" To forgive the belief in separation is
to say to God: "Show me the Union of Eternity." The Holy
Spirit will convince you that time is unreal and Eternity is
real if you will let Him. Nothing is asked of you in Truth, for
You are already and forever Perfect, Whole, and Complete
as God created You. Forgiveness opens the way to remember
this Truth.**

Love & Blessings, David

CAN ABUSE AND INNOCENCE
BE RECONCILED?

Hello David,

I have a couple of questions…

Suddenly, ACIM teachings are affecting me differently. However, I understand that we must see the innocence in our brother, and evil is only of this world. Although I understand it, I find it hard to truly accept it. How can you see the innocence in a man who has beaten and raped you? How can you give "tough love" to an individual who is hopelessly addicted to drugs and alcohol without being an enabler? You see, these are the areas where I feel blocked. Could you help me understand why there is no opposite to God, to Love? I believe that. However, the devil is the evil that men do on earth. In the Course there is no evil, no devil…or is the devil merely a synonym of perception of the ego? God does not see evil… If God does not see evil does that mean we have to accept rapists, pedophiles and murderers without judgment? Please help me understand this. Do you ever plan to come to Michigan for a gathering? I would love to meet you.

Eternal Love.

Blessings Beloved One,

Your questions go to the heart of the matter called forgiveness. I have been told by the Holy Spirit that God is All-Loving, All-Knowing, and All-Powerful. God is a God of Pure Love. This description of God is an expression of the idea: God is Love and Love has no opposite. What God creates is like God. Spirit comes from Spirit. God is Spirit. Christ is Spirit. Creation is Spirit. Innocence is an attribute of Spirit, just as Perfection and Eternity are attributes of Spirit. If evil or error were possible, Divine Innocence would be impossible. Yet because Divine Innocence is Reality, evil or error cannot be at all.

Forgiveness is for illusion, not for the Truth. Love does not need to be forgiven. In the Oneness of God there is nothing to forgive. Nothing God creates needs forgiveness, for Creation and Christ are like God in Spirit and extend God's Perfection. Forgiveness recognizes that what you think your brother has done has in Fact never happened. In ACIM it is stated this way: "If God is real there is no pain. If pain is real there is no God."(W-190.3) God is the Source of All and pain is therefore causeless and impossible. "If" there were an imposter "cause," a claim made against the Fact of the Allness of God's Love, that "cause error" would need to be released BECAUSE the error would be the denial of Divine Love.

This is why you are drawn to A Course In Miracles: you have not been able to reconcile Love with fear, Truth with illusion, or Innocence with guilt. These seeming "opposites" can NEVER be reconciled. To forgive is simply to accept the happy Fact that Truth is true and nothing else is true. To forgive is to happily release the belief in an opposite to Love. To forgive is to find the Innocence of Spirit. You humbly accept: "I am still as God created Me" as the error of separation has been forgiven.

You asked: "...is the devil merely a synonym of perception of the ego?" Yes. The ego/error/devil was Corrected by the Holy Spirit the instant the error seemed to arise. And now your only responsibility is to accept this Correction. What you believe you will perceive, as long as perception seems to last. Believe the error and you will seem to perceive abuse and addiction. Accept the Correction and you will seem to perceive a forgiven world shining in the Light of the Holy Spirit. Accept the Correction and you have given up the attempt to reconcile "opposites." Accept the Correction and lasting peace is the only possible result. Accept the Correction and see the impossibility of concepts such as "...rapists, pedophiles and murderers." This is the Last Judgment: "Holy are You, Eternal, Free, & Whole, at Peace forever in the Heart of God."

Where is the world in this Loving Judgment? The world has ended in Laughter, for what seemed to be a world apart from God was attempting to take serious a silly, mad idea of separation. Once the past is released it is as if it never was, BECAUSE it never was.

You are not alone and Help is Given you. This message, the Awakening Mind web site, the many messages on the Awakening In Christ Group, and the travels and gatherings are just some of the many witnesses to the Love you have Called forth in your awareness. The Joy I share heralds the end of illusion! The peace I experience is the peace that comes from acknowledging that Love is real and has no opposite. The Bible said to have no graven images before God. This is because God knows no images, being Pure Spirit. Forgive the images that never were, and experience indescribable Happiness!

The dreamer of a dream first realizes the dreaming. Nothing can hurt the dreamer once the Holy Spirit has revealed the dream as unreal. Without judgment all dream figures are the same, for it was only the ego that made up the categories of victim and victimizer, abused and abuser, enabled and enabler to perpetuate itself. Once the ego is released, perception has been healed, and nothing blocks the way to the experience of God's Divine Love.

All Glory to the Living God! Love Always, David

RELEASING THE FEAR OF
SPECIAL LOVE WITH A TEACHER

Dear David,

Thank you for your response to my message. I have tried to follow your suggestions and I have talked to several others about this. None of them have helped me to see how this was really for my greatest good. I have also let some time pass by hoping that time would be a great healer. In this case it hasn't because even today I was still driven to more tears over all of this.

I AM NOW AFRAID TO:
1) Trust any teacher of God that they will act in my best interests.
2) Enter into any kind of relationship Holy or otherwise for fear that the Holy Spirit (God) will reject me.
3) Open myself up to a vulnerable state like I did for fear that I will be crushed again.
4) Trust anyone's guidance including my own that it is actually the Holy Spirit that is guiding them.
5) Trust that the Course principles will be followed by apparent teachers of God.

...So far your answers are helpful in a general way but do not enable me to solve this mystery. Solving mysteries may be an ego quality but the main thing here is the following. If the holy spirit was in control of this relationship why did it result in fear not love?

Blessings.

Beloved One,

Thanks for your e-mail and your little willingness for healing. God Wills Perfect Happiness and the ego is the belief in mysteries and questions and secrets. In Light is

everything openly revealed, and thus it must be that to the ego Revelation is fearful. Fear but seems to be about "persons" "places" and "things," but fear of God's Love is the strange belief that must be exposed and seen as false. Your "relationship" with your brother was a step in facing the fear within, for nothing of this world of images is fearful. Your brief encounter with your brother was a way of bringing to awareness what lies beneath. This fear of God must come up to be released, and the contact with your brother served that Purpose. Healing is the goal of all mind training, and one cannot release what is kept in unawareness.

Hurt and loss seem real only because of the belief in a break in communication. I faced this illusion and with the Guidance of the Holy Spirit came to see that communication from God cannot be broken. No body or worldly event or situation or circumstance can break the Love God offers always. Love must come through the mind to be experienced by the mind, and the only seeming experience of pain results from the belief that Love can be withheld. It cannot. In the world of form "love" and "communication" can seem to be broken, but nothing of the world is true. Forgiveness releases, the ego binds. All seeming "relationships" mirror the need to release the ego until it is apparent that the ego was never real. This points to the Atonement, the awareness that God and Christ are the only real Relationship. Union is of the Christ Mind, Which is Communion – the Communication of Creator and Creation.

Jesus devotes nine chapters to "special relationships" in ACIM and says that the special love relationship is the ego's most boasted "gift." (T-16.V.3) The undoing of the guilt and fear and pain of specialness is only painful to the ego, which is being undone. Yet you are opening to the awareness that you ARE NOT the ego. You are Holy. The Holy bless and offer only blessing, so nothing can be lost in extending the Self God creates Perfect.

The Holy Spirit leads through the darkness to the Light. The "journey inward" may seem "dark" to the ego, for the ego is being undone and it resents and fears each step. I am joined with you in coming through the perceived fear. No "body" can increase fear, yet while you give faith to the ego you will value bodies and the communication from bodies.

I share with you a Communication that can never be broken off, for I offer what the Holy Spirit shares with you. This inner blessing is not dependent on words, yet I use them Now to encourage you to go through the fear within to the Love that is still deeper within.

If the Holy Spirit's Purpose is held firmly as the only goal, I assure you that only Love can be the experience. An "experience" of fear is a Call for Love, a Call to extend what was believed to be lacking. This extension can never be blocked. "Relationships" only reflect belief, and if "a relationship with your brother" seemed to be broken it only reflected the belief that the Relationship with God had been broken. Love is unbreakable and indivisible. Ask if the ego's belief and misperception could ever satisfy your holy mind, and realize You have the Answer.

Do not look to "another" for Guidance. The external "seeking" was the seeming sickness of mind. You have the Truth within our Mind. Seek within and you shall find What is forever true. The ego teaches that relationships begin and end, rejoicing in the former and lamenting the latter. Nothing that is True has a "beginning" or an "end." Glory be to the Living One for creating Love Eternal!!!

I love You forever and ever! David

SEXUAL ABUSE ISSUES

Hi David,

In my meditative state I sometimes am drawn to do forgiveness exercises using the lesson "God is the love in which I forgive _____." In these exercises my grandfather and uncle have come up in relation to sexual abuse. I proceed as usual in forgiving them and myself. I have no specific memories of abuse. I also have very little memories of life before about 6 years old. So if these events occurred they may have been very early.

So how can I work in removing these blocks to love's presence? I also have a memory of around 12 years old when I witnessed my brother and his friends having sexual relations with a young girl. I presume I felt some guilt from this even though I did not participate. I also have some vague memory of some sexual contact with my sister, probably at about 8 years old. Is there anything specific I can do about these memories?

Thanks.

Beloved One,

Thanks for writing. Sexual attraction and sexual abuse seem very different to the mind asleep and dreaming, and to the ego, attraction is often judged as positive and abuse as negative. Yet anything that is used to reinforce the "reality" of the body in awareness is an attempt to deny the Reality of Spirit. Memories are interpretations from the past that are called forth and experienced as if they are still present. Past associations can seem to offer pleasure or pain, and the sameness of these seemingly different experiences must be recognized before they can be released as one error. In forgiveness the misperception of abuse is gone, for there is no longer a belief in opposites.

The perception of a grievance requires a victim and a victimizer, and this perception, forgiveness cannot perceive. The projection of attack thoughts produced the illusory interpretation of abuse. Once the projection is seen as the attempt to keep the attack thoughts, this defense will no longer seem helpful. Peace comes from the release of attack thoughts, and thus all ego attempts to repress or project attack thoughts are only ways of blocking inner peace from awareness.

There is a Perspective of the body and world that offers only blessings. This is holy relationship. The body is seen as a symbol of communication and has no value in and of itself. What is the body for? "Does it serve the Light?" is the only helpful question in any situation in which the thought of bodies has entered. Let the Spirit smile and laugh and hug through the body, and you will see the body in the Light of forgiveness. In this Light there is neither attraction or repulsion, for what is wholly neutral can merely serve the One Who brings healing. In this Purpose is the experience of Joy. Joy is ever fulfilling and offers the Perspective that all things work together for good. Glory to God!

Love, David

CONFUSION AROUND SEXUALITY

Greetings David,

I have been reading a course in miracles for 6 months and am also doing the lessons in the workbook. When I received this book I knew that the words within its covers were meant to be read by me, and its message resounds clearly with the light within. I know that the words in this course speak the truth and more important to my happiness than anything else is that I fulfill my part in God's plan for salvation.

However I am particularly confused about the area of sexuality at the moment. I find myself in a situation where I am being offered a sexual relationship with a married man who is also sexually involved with a friend who lives in the same house as me. This appears to be a particularly complicated situation. Recently I admitted to this man that I was attempting to avoid the physical pain I experienced in sex by not getting involved in a sexual relationship. He offered me the chance to be with him – as someone who trusted that I could have a pain-free experience and who was willing to be patient in looking for that experience with me.

I accepted his offer and found that I was willing to express the pain in front of him instead of trying to hide it (which I had done in previous relationships) and that once we talked openly about it I was able to have a sexual experience that was pain free. This was quite an intense experience for me and when he spent the following night with my house mate I found fear coming to the surface. I doubted that there had actually been a meeting of anything other than two egos when we were together and that he was simply out to 'get whatever he could.' I am confused by the fact that I am being offered this experience with a man who is now sexually involved with 3 different women and married to one of them. It is very hard to believe that there is no judgment placed upon me for getting involved in such a situation. I am also finding it difficult to maintain a friendship with my house mate when we are both involved with the same man.

It seems that I have just opened a part of my mind that I had sought to keep firmly apart from the rest until recently and it appears to have resulted in much confusion! As the course is all about relationships I am sure that this is a gift to all of us involved in this strange situation, but at the same time I consider the possibility that I am just deluding myself into believing that I want something other than the truth.

I would be so grateful to hear some words from you, brother.

Beloved One,

Thanks for sharing what is on your heart. The ego is flushed up and exposed in relationships, and aligning with the ego brings illusory experiences of pleasure and pain. Distorted miracle impulses reach awareness as cravings, and in this regard sexual cravings are the same as cravings for food, drink, temperature, stimulation, etc. Cravings always involve lack and preferences, and the miracle leads past this distorted perception of the world. As the ego belief system is questioned and exposed and released the "lens of lack" is cleared of all obstacles to peace. When this happens miracle impulses are experienced directly in awareness as Love and Calls for Love.

Wholeness and completion are the natural characteristics of the mind, and the miracle returns these characteristics to awareness. Complexity is always of the ego. The ego uses relationships for gratification and the ego, being impulsive and unstable, has no conception of commitment. Commitment to a monogamous interpersonal relationship is a step that the Holy Spirit can use (as with any commitment or discipline) to open the mind to the sole or ultimate commitment that one can make: accepting the Atonement or Awakening to God's

Love. I have referred to the ego's purpose for relationships as "Dixie cup relationships." The ego seems to throw its relationships away once it seems to get what it thinks it wants and moves on to the next relationship for another drink.

Simultaneous sexual relationships or "open" relationships as they have been called seem to add to the complexity. A monogamous interpersonal relationship can offer a full plate of opportunities to expose and forgive the ego, and the undoing of the ego (forgiveness) is the only Purpose for all relationships. The ultimate realization (Self-realization) is the recognition that Creator and Creation share the same Spirit of Love. At best all perceptual relationships reflect the Love of God, and this Agape Love inspires forgiveness and miracles.

The Holy Spirit Guides surely. Simplicity is of God, and the illusion of complexity is the error to be forgiven.

Love always, David

SEXUALITY AND DESIRE

Dear David,

The Course doesn't say anything about sex, as if it didn't exist. But it very much exists for me. I'm gay (though not presently in a relationship) and I've been interested in "Sacred Sexuality" for some time.

Having no sexual partner, I arouse myself to orgasm on my own a few times a week and thanks to the books I've read I consider it to be a sacred act. As I move deeper into the heart of ACIM I'm noticing that more and more often I simply have lost interest in sex. It doesn't bother me – usually my thought is, "Oh, good, I'll have more time for other things now."

My questions are:

1. Should sex just be ignored as apparently ACIM does?
2. Should students like me enjoy it until its attractiveness evaporates away?
3. Is there anything really "sacred" in the sex act, and should I use it, as one Sacred Sex book puts it, as a springboard to transcendence?
4. And finally, if I decide to ignore my sex drives and live a life of abstinence and celibacy, will the repression of those sex drives cause any problems? I'm inclined towards celibacy but that's because my Catholic upbringing made sex a mortal sin punishable by eternity in Hell. That clearly is not the right motivation to take a vow of celibacy.

Thanks for your help with this, David. Much Love.

Beloved One,

Thanks for your direct questions about sexuality. What you do comes from what you think, and that is why Awakening is a purification of thought. Behavior modification is therefore never the goal, for behavior but follows the guide the mind chooses to listen to and follow. Sexual desire is not better or worse than any desire for the world, yet Awakening is a state of contentment that is desireless. This is the Peace that passeth the understanding of the world. All appetites are ego getting mechanisms, and fantasy is the attempt to make false associations and obtain pleasure from them.

As the miracle expands and becomes consistently experienced, these appetites fade, grow dim, and disappear. The ego was the belief in lack, and all apparent appetites reflected this belief. The ego attempted to put various behaviors into moral and ethical systems of judgment, yet in the healed Perspective only Wholeness is experienced and the past is gone. There is no hierarchy of illusions, no order of difficulty in miracles, and no preferences in the Atonement. The ego was one error and cannot be broken into "enjoyable" error and "punishable" error, "moral" error and "immoral" error, "ethical" error and "unethical" error. Celibacy and monogamy and masturbation are all stepping-stone concepts along the path of emptying the mind of all concepts, forgiving the illusion, and Awakening to Pure Oneness. Sacred sexuality is a contradiction in terms because Spirit transcends form entirely and it is impossible to mix Spirit and matter.

Pleasure and pain are the same error. The miracle transcends the error by showing its falsity, its impossibility. It is impossible to seek for pleasure without finding pain, for both are the same error: the attempt to reinforce the "reality" of the body and world. Christ is Spirit, not a body, and to experience Divine Mind is to forget the body entirely. At no single instant does the body exist at all. It is always remembered (past) or anticipated (future) in dreaming. This is the error of linear time. As one experiences the Holy Instant, the experience of bodies and time are no more.

Awakening involves mind training. Pay attention to the thoughts that come into awareness. Detach. Desire healing. Preferences are judgments, and as the mind yields to the Nonjudgmental Perspective of the Holy Spirit the Awakening is obvious. You will observe that as long as appetites seem to exist there are the ego defenses of indulgence and repression. Neither is better or worse than the other, for they are the same illusion.

The miracle offers a real alternative, and when one is consistently miracle-minded, defenses are no longer needed. Let the Holy Spirit Guide you in the moment to the experience of the Holy Instant. In the Holy Instant God is Known, Christ is Known, and "sexuality" is unknown and unknowable. The perceptual world disappears in the Thought of God. The Thought of God is Sacred. Christ is Spirit. God is Spirit. That which is born of the Spirit is Spirit. Such is the simple Truth.

Love & Blessings, David

THE STEPPING STONES OF AWAKENING IN ACIM

Dear David,

I just cannot understand these statements in ACIM. Would you please throw some light on these? You might say that words are symbols twice removed from reality. But what other choice do I have other than to request that you answer them in something that I can relate to? I do not know of any other experience other than mundane worldly experience.

Lesson 135
"...Yet it is not the body that can fear nor be a thing of fear. It has no needs but those which you assign to it. It needs no complicated structures of defense, no health inducing medicine, no care and no concern at all...."

But we still have to feed it water, food for sustaining it, is it not? No matter how I think, I cannot understand this.

Lesson 132
"...There is no world. This is the central thought the course attempts to teach. Not everyone is ready to accept it, and each one must go as far as he can let himself be led along the road to truth. He will return and go still further, or perhaps step back a while and then return again..."

Does this not point to re-incarnation? It says not everyone is ready to accept it. Yet ACIM says Heaven cannot be reached alone and you have to take everyone with you. Does it mean that those who are ready will only enter heaven and others will have to remain here and work towards it? If Jesus or Buddha attained heaven how come we are still here? How could they reach without me for example? This also is beyond comprehension because it is contradictory. I am immensely grateful for all your help.

Thanking you.

Beloved One,

Thanks for writing and sharing your sincere questions. The first quotation points to the teaching that the seeming "source" of fear and need is the false "cause," the belief in separation in the mind, and has nothing to do with the body. The ego belief is a wrong-minded decision to project fear and needs to the body, as if the body and the environment that seems to surround the body can be "causes" of fear. Needs and fears arise from the sense of lack that the belief in separation induces. You might say that the only need the sleeping mind has is to accept the Atonement or Correction for the belief in separation. The ego attempts to protect itself by making it seem as if the fears and needs are in the cosmos and the body, yet images are neutral to the Holy Spirit, and images can neither fear or have needs.

Until the mind is Awakened through retraining via the Holy Spirit, it will seem as if there are causes in the world. Hunger, thirst, sexual desire, and the desire for stimulation seem to be based in the body and brain, yet they arise from distorted miracle impulses that pass through the lens of lack. All fears and cravings and needs are wrong-minded perceptions, yet answering the Call to be a miracle worker will yield many miracles and dissolve the lens of lack. Until the lens of lack is dissolved completely, the sleeping mind will experience cravings, and cravings are either acted upon and temporarily satisfied, or pushed down and denied from awareness. Neither approach will satisfy in a lasting way, yet miracles open the door to lasting Peace and Joy and Freedom and Happiness. In miracles are all seeming human needs met without effort. And the final miracle of Atonement brings an end to the belief in need and lack and fear, forever.

The second quotation points toward the realization that there is no objective world/cosmos apart from the sleeping mind (ego), and since the ego does not exist, neither does the world/cosmos it seemed to produce. Mind Awake is Christ, eternally in the Mind of God. The Mind of God is Reality and there is nothing "outside" of the all-encompassing Mind of God. Spirit is Eternal and the time-space cosmos is but an illusory dream that has no existence or reality. The perceived world/cosmos was made by the ego, yet the ego is nothing. It is subjective in that everything which appears as the dream is given pseudo meaning by the ego that made it.

The Holy Spirit offers the Perspective of a forgiven world in which all distortions have been straightened out, or neutralized. This Perspective is the gateway to Eternity, for this Perspective is one of non-judgment. Judgment makes the world/cosmos hallucination seem real to the perceiver, while forgiveness shows the falsity of the world/cosmos. Everyone wakes up as One because the realization dawns that there are no private thoughts or private minds, no individual persons or separate individual "souls," nothing that "comes to" or "leaves" a cosmos that never was.

The Vision of Christ is Pure Light and in this Light the veil of images that seemed to be the world/cosmos has vanished. Jesus is a symbol of a man who saw the face of Christ and remembered the Eternal Oneness of Heaven, or Nirvana. Now is the time to accept that You are that same One, and realize that it is impossible to be even a "spiritual person," for God is no respecter of persons. Mind cannot be broken into separate bits of consciousness and given separate names and roles and meanings. The role model of an "awakened master" is helpful only to a certain step, and then it finally dawns that OneSelf IS the Living One. You are included in the Awakening because forgiveness is unified mind. In the forgiven world it is apparent that there is nothing outside the mind. The world/cosmos was a mind of ideas, and all of mind is included in forgiveness.

Stay devoted to the experience of Awakening through forgiveness, and push off and lay aside the stepping stones which are naturally released as higher awareness dawns. Your desire for God will bring the remembrance of God, and nothing is capable of preventing this inevitable Realization. I love You dearly Beloved Child of God. We are the same One.

Love always, David

STEWARDSHIP PART 1

Blessings of Joy and Love! Glory to the One Who is the Giver of Life Eternal. I have been asked to speak on the topic of Stewardship by my sisters and brothers, and so I shall.

Stewardship has its Source in God, Who is the Giver of Life. In relation to this world, the mind believes it has forgotten God and is imagining a sense of incompletion and lack. The sleeping mind believes in needs and wants and seeks for abilities and things and people to satisfy these desires. The Holy Spirit meets these perceived desires as the mind Awakens, teaching the mind to release all false beliefs and concepts that made up the perceived needs and desires. Such is Stewardship. It is stepping back and allowing the Holy Spirit to take care of all the "details" of Awakening. The Holy Spirit leads to an experience of Wholeness and Completion in which there is no lack. As the sleeping mind begins to trust, the Holy Spirit's miracles light the way, for they show the truth of the idea "I am sustained by the Love of God."

Stewardship is always voluntary, just as Awakening is voluntary. Unless the use of mind effort (time and skills and resources and funds and energy) is entirely voluntary there will be a sense of coercion and a host of "shoulds" "ought to's" "musts" and "have to's." A steward uses what is available in the service of the Holy Spirit's Purpose and comes to experience that Giving and Receiving are the same. The Purpose channels all effort in one direction; Atonement or Complete Forgiveness, and this is how perception is integrated and healed of every distortion.

Those who are Called to Stewardship have been Asked to step into their function. Whatever they seemed to possess in this world is given over to a new Purpose that will show them that it is God which provides and sustains, and ultimately that there is nothing apart from Life in God. From deep within, one is Called to this holy function. The only question is whether one will choose to listen to, answer, follow, and fulfill this Call. "I am Calling you out of the world" is the same Call that has remained constant under the shifting world of conflict and scarcity.

Here are some parables about the blocks to Stewardship taken from the back of *The Urantia Book*. A steward is one who is willing to volunteer for the opportunity to serve God by forgiving, and thus releasing all attachments to the world. As a context for these parables, Jesus and his apostles are training disciples to share the teachings and good news of the Heavenly Kingdom:

One earnest disciple came to Jesus, saying: "Master, I would be one of your new apostles, but my father is very old and near death; could I be permitted to return home to bury him?" To this man Jesus said: "My son, the foxes have holes, and the birds of heaven have nests, but the Son of Man has nowhere to lay his head. You are a faithful disciple, and you can remain such while you return home to minister to your loved ones, but not so with my gospel messengers. They have forsaken all to follow me and proclaim the Kingdom. If you would be an ordained teacher, you must let others bury the dead while you go forth to publish the good news." And this man went away in great disappointment.

Another disciple came to the Master and said: "I would become an ordained messenger, but I would like to go to my home for a short while to comfort my family." And Jesus replied: "If you would be ordained, you must be willing to forsake all. The gospel messengers cannot have divided affections. No man, having put his hand to the plough, if he turns back, is worthy to become a messenger of the Kingdom."

Then Andrew brought to Jesus a certain rich young man who was a devout believer, and who desired to receive ordination. This young man, Matadormus, was a member of the Jerusalem Sanhedrin; he had heard Jesus teach and had been subsequently instructed in the gospel of the Kingdom by Peter and the other apostles. Jesus talked with Matadormus concerning the requirements of ordination and requested that he defer decision until after he had thought more fully about the matter. Early the next morning, as Jesus was going for a walk, this young man accosted him and said: "Master, I would know from you the assurances of eternal life. Seeing that I have observed all the commandments from my youth, I would like to know what more I must do to gain eternal life?" In answer to this question Jesus said: "If you keep all the commandments – do not commit adultery, do not kill, do not steal, do not bear false witness, do not defraud, honor your parents – you do well, but salvation is the reward of faith, not merely of works. Do you believe this gospel of the Kingdom?" And Matadormus answered: "Yes, Master, I do believe everything you and your apostles have taught me." And Jesus said, "Then are you indeed my disciple and a child of the Kingdom."

Then said the young man: "But, Master, I am not content to be your disciple; I would be one of your new messengers." When Jesus heard this, he looked down upon him with a great love and said: "I will have you to be one of my messengers if you are willing to pay the price, if you will supply the one thing which you lack." Matadormus replied: "Master, I will do anything if I may be allowed to follow you." Jesus, kissing the kneeling young man on the forehead, said: "If you would be my messenger, go and sell all that you have and, when you have bestowed the proceeds upon the poor or upon your brethren, come and follow me, and you shall have treasure in the Kingdom of heaven."

When Matadormus heard this, his countenance fell. He arose and went away sorrowful, for he had great possessions. This wealthy young Pharisee had been raised to believe that wealth was the token of God's favor. Jesus knew that he was not free from the love of himself and his riches. The Master wanted to deliver him from the love of wealth, not necessarily from the wealth. While the disciples of Jesus did not part with all their worldly goods, the apostles and the seventy did. Matadormus desired to be one of the seventy new messengers, and that was the reason for Jesus' requiring him to part with all of his temporal possessions.

Almost every human being has some one thing which is held on to as a pet evil, and which the entrance into the Kingdom of heaven requires as a part of the price of admission. If Matadormus had parted with his wealth, it probably would have been put right back into his hands for administration as treasurer of the seventy. For later on, after the establishment of the church at Jerusalem, he did obey the Master's injunction, although it was then too late to enjoy membership in the seventy, and he became the treasurer of the Jerusalem church, of which James the Lord's brother in the flesh was the head.

Thus always it was and forever will be: Men must arrive at their own decisions. There is a certain range of the freedom of choice which mortals may exercise. The forces of the spiritual world will not coerce man; they allow him to go the way of his own choosing. (Urantia, part IV

Jesus foresaw that Matadormus, with his riches, could not possibly become an ordained associate of men who had forsaken all for the gospel; at the same time, he saw that, without his riches, he would become the ultimate leader of all of them. ...Riches have nothing directly to do with entrance into the Kingdom of heaven, but the love of wealth does. The spiritual loyalties of the Kingdom are incompatible with servility to materialistic mammon. Man may not share his supreme loyalty to a spiritual ideal with a material devotion.

Stewardship has its basis in Divine Providence and can be summarized as "God takes Care." Over the years this idea has been expressed in many ways. Jesus said "Take

no thought for tomorrow," "Take no thought for what you should wear or eat," and "Seek ye first the Kingdom of Heaven, and all else shall be added unto you." In A Course In Miracles Christ expresses the idea this way:

"You may wonder how you can be at peace when, while you are in time, there is so much that must be done before the way to peace is open. Perhaps this seems impossible to you. But ask yourself if it is possible that God would have a plan for your salvation that does not work. Once you accept His plan as the one function that you would fulfill, there will be nothing else the Holy Spirit will not arrange for you without your effort. He will go before you making straight your path, and leaving in your way no stones to trip on, and no obstacles to bar your way. Nothing you need will be denied you. Not one seeming difficulty but will melt away before you reach it. You need take thought for nothing, careless of everything except the only purpose that you would fulfill. As that was given you, so will its fulfillment be. God's guarantee will hold against all obstacles, for it rests on certainty and not contingency." (T-20.IV.8) This is a Promise that, when sincerely followed, bears much fruit.

In the Psychotherapy Pamphlet it is expressed like this:

No one can pay for therapy, for healing is of God and He asks for nothing. It is, however, part of His plan that everything in this world be used by the Holy Spirit to help in carrying out the plan. Even an advanced therapist has some earthly needs while he is here. Should he need money it will be given him, not in payment, but to help him better serve the plan. Money is not evil. It is nothing. But no one here can live with no illusions, for he must yet strive to have the last illusion be accepted by everyone everywhere. He has a mighty part in this one purpose, for which he came. He stays here but for this. And while he stays he will be given what he needs to stay.

Only an unhealed healer would try to heal for money,

and he will not succeed to the extent to which he values it. Nor will he find his healing in the process. There will be those of whom the Holy Spirit asks some payment for His purpose. There will be those from whom He does not ask. It should not be the therapist who makes these decisions. There is a difference between payment and cost. To give money where God's plan allots it has no cost. To withhold it from where it rightfully belongs has enormous cost. The therapist who would do this loses the name of healer, for he could never understand what healing is. He cannot give it, and so he does not have it.

The therapists of this world are indeed useless to the world's salvation. They make demands, and so they cannot give. Patients can pay only for the exchange of illusions. This, indeed, must demand payment, and the cost is great. A "bought" relationship cannot offer the only gift whereby all healing is accomplished. Forgiveness, the Holy Spirit's only dream, must have no cost. For if it does, it merely crucifies God's Son again. Can this be how he is forgiven? Can this be how the dream of sin will end?

The right to live is something no one need fight for. It is promised him, and guaranteed by God. Therefore it is a right the therapist and patient share alike. If their relationship is to be holy, whatever one needs is given by the other; whatever one lacks the other supplies. Herein is the relationship made holy, for herein both are healed. The therapist repays the patient in gratitude, as does the patient repay him. There is no cost to either. But thanks are due to both, for the release from long imprisonment and doubt. Who would not be grateful for such a gift? Yet who could possibly imagine that it could be bought?

It has well been said that to him who hath shall be given. Because he has, he can give. And because he gives, he shall be given. This is the law of God, and not of the world. So it is with God's healers. They give because they have heard His Word and understood it. All that they need will thus be given them. But they will lose this understanding unless they remember that all they have comes only from God. If they believe they need anything from a brother, they will recognize him as a brother no longer. And if they do this, a light goes out even in Heaven. Where God's Son turns against himself, he can look only upon darkness. He has himself denied the light, and cannot see.

One rule should always be observed: No one should be turned away because he cannot pay. No one is sent by accident to anyone. Relationships are always purposeful. Whatever their purpose may have been before the Holy Spirit entered them, they are always His potential temple; the resting place of Christ and home of God Himself. Whoever comes has been sent. Perhaps he was sent to give his brother the money he needed. Both will be blessed thereby. Perhaps he was sent to teach the therapist how much he needs forgiveness, and how valueless is money in comparison. Again will both be blessed. Only in terms of cost could one have more. In sharing, everyone must gain a blessing without cost.

This view of payment may well seem impractical, and in the eyes of the world it would be so. Yet not one worldly thought is really practical. How much is gained by striving for illusions? How much is lost by throwing God away? And is it possible to do so? Surely it is impractical to strive for nothing, and to attempt to do what is impossible. Then stop a while, long enough to think of this: You have perhaps been seeking for salvation without recognizing where to look. Whoever asks your help can show you where. What greater gift than this could you be given? What greater gift is there that you would give?

Physician, healer, therapist, teacher, heal thyself. Many will come to you carrying the gift of healing, if you so elect. The Holy Spirit never refuses an invitation to enter and abide with you. He will give you endless opportuni-

ties to open the door to your salvation, for such is His function. He will also tell you exactly what your function is in every circumstance and at all times. Whoever He sends you will reach you, holding out his hand to his Friend. Let the Christ in you bid him welcome, for that same Christ is in him as well. Deny him entrance, and you have denied the Christ in you. Remember the sorrowful story of the world, and the glad tidings of salvation. Remember the plan of God for the restoration of joy and peace. And do not forget how very simple are the ways of God: You were lost in the darkness of the world until you asked for light. And then God sent His Son to give it to you. (P3.III.1-8)

The message of Awakening I share has unfolded under the names "Messengers of Peace" and "Foundation for the Awakening Mind." The foundation is a nonprofit unincorporated organization dedicated to sharing the teaching materials that point to a State of Enlightenment.

Through the Grace of God and in the Name of God I, and those who have been Guided to join in, are honored to serve and reflect the One in offering writings, audio & video clips, gatherings, CDs, mp3s, DVDs, books, e-mails, journal offerings, video-gatherings, counseling sessions, phone sessions, quiet retreats, and Internet ministry, all of which help shed light on the experience of forgiveness. These offerings are available without charge to those who request them. Awakening to Who You Are has no price or cost. Love offering gifts and donations are gratefully accepted. We welcome all inquiries and requests from anyone with a deep, sincere desire to Awaken to Eternal Love. Always feel free to send a letter or an e-mail and feel free to call and speak with one of us or leave a voice message.

Divine Providence is the Source of Sustenance in serving the Plan of Awakening to Joy. I see that the travels and gatherings and work with brothers and sisters from all over the world have all been orchestrated by the Holy Spirit in the Plan of

Awakening. I attribute all "earthly forms" of support to the Holy Spirit, for truly the Miracle is the means to Awakening and the Miracle encompasses all. The forms have seemed to be many and varied. Freely I have received of God, and freely I give what I have received.

The mission continues Now, inspired by the Holy Spirit's Purpose. Jesus of Nazareth lives in our hearts. Freely Christ has given the Gospel to live and to give, and freely I extend the Gift. It is an honor and a joy to share the Love of God, and as Jesus once said: "The messenger is worth his keep." Everything I have ever thought I needed in serving God's Plan has been provided. Holy Spirit watches over the Plan, and I am assured that this Watchful Care continues as long as any need is experienced. He has been with us always as we carry on our simple mission. Whatever we have seemed to need, be it a car, a meal, a place to stay, or a calm, gentle reminder, all our needs have been met by Him. There is a calmness of heart in turning all perceived problems and needs over to Him and listening for His sure Guidance. The resurrection of Christ is the risen Christ, Awakened in God's Love.

The Foundation for the Awakening Mind, which oversees all operations and distributes the teaching materials, offers everything freely and extends the materials far and wide across the earth. We receive and answer requests from countries all over the planet. The foundation has always accepted donations offered in loving support of Christ's mission. Recently several people have expressed an interest in organizing Stewardship support for the foundation's mission. The most often asked question about this task is: What is the foundation and what are the stated purpose and activities of the foundation? These questions are answered simply in the foundation's bylaws:

> *The Foundation for the Awakening Mind is a non-membership organization. Anyone and everyone with a desire to teach and learn true forgiveness, lay aside grievances and judgments, and to live and extend inner peace may*

consider themselves a member of our corporation. All contributions of time, resources, skills, and service to the goal of inner peace are welcome and gratefully received. We are organized for religious and educational purposes, for we understand forgiveness is Divinely inspired and must be thoroughly taught and learned to be experienced. We are not, however, affiliated with any religious denomination or educational institution. Our organization aims at a transformation of consciousness to inner peace, and thus we seek to remove all mental blocks and barriers that prevent the awareness of love. All are included in the experience of inner peace. We teach and learn that we all hold membership in the Family of God, the Family of Peace.

Purpose: The Foundation for the Awakening Mind is a nonprofit Educational Foundation established for the purpose of teaching and learning true forgiveness, laying aside all grievances, and living and extending inner peace. First and foremost, we shall encourage prayer, meditation, and miracles – the laying aside of judgment – as the means of achieving the learning goal.

Everything is simply a backdrop for Awakening for those that are attracted to the Divine Purpose of the Holy Spirit. Every seeming holy encounter is an opportunity to accept complete forgiveness and extend inner peace. Everyone who joins this mighty Purpose serves the Holy Spirit and is served by the Holy Spirit. My Purpose I share with All: Teach only Love, for that is What You are.

Love, David

STEWARDSHIP PART 2

Dear Davidji,

Thank you, the answer to my question on stewardship has been answered in Part 1 of Stewardship. One has been drawn towards the Awakening Mind Organization. We have spoken of this. Nothing seems to be happening towards this manifesting. There seem to be "road blocks" on the way. Is this my own ego mind and its shenanigans? One doesn't want to "lose" like some of the seekers who wanted to join Jesus' messenger group. When this feeling of loss appears before one, it feels like one is losing out on the Kingdom of heaven. At this point some illusion seems to be getting "mixed up" with the Reality. It's a very strange paradox occurring. Yet underneath it all there is a wisdom that what is to occur will occur.

But then how much longer to wait before the wings of the Dove pick this form up and take it to where it belongs? Flummoxed and calm at the same time yet so wanting to remain true to Purpose and the Holy Spirit… Help!!!! In Love and Oneness with Him who is the only truth…

I love you forever.

Beloved One,

Thanks for your deep devotion to Awakening! If you hold the Holy Spirit's Purpose out front as the top priority, everything will unfold in a very easy, obvious manner. You will watch it all unfold effortlessly and in Joy, because you have no investment in outcome, and are voluntarily taking every step with the Holy Spirit. You are always welcome in my heart and I feel you may someday come and live at the Journey's End Retreat Center.

It is a Joy to watch all those who come forward to witness to Divine Love as they trust and take the steps that are Given to them by the Holy Spirit. The invitations come so easily, and it is a Joy to accept each one. There is no reciprocity, or bargaining, or exchange in Divine Providence, and this trust dissolves the ego entirely. In Awakening there is no loss or sacrifice. The ego was the belief in sacrifice, yet its nothingness cannot be a real "roadblock" to Awakening because Awakening shows that there is no ego. Love is real and has no opposite. All Glory to the One for creating Love as It is forevermore!

Love, David

STUCK.
LOOKING FOR A SPIRITUAL HOME

David,

I'm a Buddhist monk, though lately I've found myself returning to a Christ consciousness. I'm not really interested in a
specific religion, being more of a generic mystic. Buddhism of
the Tibetan variety used to be a path with heart, now I don't
think so, though the problem may be more with the leadership,
than with the path itself. So, my question; I've been looking for
a spiritual home for about a year and seem to be stuck. Also,
I've been living in Ecuador for two years, though I know
that I am needed there, I'm not sure how much longer I can
endure the inertia in that culture, I seem to lack the wisdom
to move forward.

With prayers and blessings.

Beloved One,

**Thanks for sharing what is on your heart. It sounds as if you
are ready to take the next step inward. If there seems to be a
struggle with the "leadership" of your path or the "culture"
that seems to surround you, this is the call to recognize that
these are thoughts that no longer serve your peace of mind. In
the Living Moment there are no leaders or followers, and the
culture you perceive is not the cause of the feeling of inertia.
Inertia is a form of the error of wishing things were different
than they are. The ego mind becomes aligned and identified
with a role or part, and this false identity becomes familiar
and comfortable. It seems to require an effort to release
these associations and assumptions for they seem more real
than the "unknown" Christ. Awakening is the seeming surrender of everything that seems to be "known" about this**

world. True religion is the experience of Peace and cannot be organized or structured at all. As all beliefs in control and organization and structure are released, the only awareness that remains is Being.

Meditation is an excellent path to detachment from false belief and thought. Travel is another excellent tool for exposing and detaching from preferences and expectations which arise from false belief. Stay with the feeling of inertia, move through it, and accept the Gift that Shines beneath it. The mind is asking for permission to experience the energy of the Divine Flow. This is your passion at heart. This is your Joy. Allow this experience into awareness and the next step will be obvious.

Blessings abound, David

TAKING THE NEXT STEP

Hi Dave,

Thank you for your latest reply. I am still, however, in a state of concern for the direction of my life, career-wise, on a personal level and in relationships. Career-wise, I am applying for various positions, not really knowing which direction to throw myself... and I am also contemplating writing a book, which I have been wanting to do, for a long time... about self-discovery.

On a personal level, I'm on lesson 105, God's peace and joy are mine... I still have trouble or resistance to sitting down and quieting my mind enough to hear and feel the messages of the Holy Spirit. I know that I am still holding on to past hurt and I keep handing it over to HS and am still affected by it... And, in relationships, I am having a hard time being real with others, telling exactly what I think instead of being a people-pleaser. I realize that this is so, in a way, because I am still not real with myself, some things I really do not like about myself. For instance, how I try to manipulate my environment in order for it to respond the way I want it to... but it doesn't always respond the way I want.

Another thing that has been preoccupying me is the whole notion of giving and receiving... I want to do my part in the illumination of the planet and do not know what that is... I don't even know who I am. Giving and receiving for me – I am starting to see this in a different light along with ACIM teachings. I am now seeing that if I am fearful and filled with judgment on myself and others then that is what I perceive and experience from within and from my environment. And if I have loving thoughts about myself and others (which does not happen very often), then that is what I am giving to the universe and am thus experiencing. I thank you, in advance for your guided response and pray that this response will be heard, listened to and felt by me... and that I will be open and receptive enough to allow for this experience to pierce through the clouds of worry, illusions that hide the Truth within...

Love

Hello Beloved One,

Thanks for your e-mail and for sharing your thoughts and concerns. The Holy Spirit is Guiding you steadfastly inward toward our shared Purpose, and past goals and pursuits that will no longer serve you on your path. The most important question to ask about the perceived aspects of your experience i.e., career-wise, on a personal level, and in relationships is "What is it for?" What is the Purpose of a career? What is the Purpose of the persona or mask I hold up to please others? What is the Purpose of relationships in my world? What is the Purpose for the book I want to write? These questions are helpful in exposing the ego belief system because they aim at discovering the underlying beliefs which motivate all behavior.

Everything in this world of form seemed to have a different purpose, or function. Therefore purpose did not seem unified and there appeared to be a variety of goals. Such was confusion. Such was complexity. Such was the past. Such was all the perceived hurt. This was the world which seemed to arise in the darkened glass of ego perception. Awakening to the Holy Spirit's Perspective (Now) requires a willingness to apply the same Purpose to every seemingly separate aspect of perception: everything and everyone and every situation. Peace of mind comes from holding a single Purpose in mind, for it is single Purpose that unifies perception. Fragmented, distorted perception came from multiple desires and goals.

The ego used the body and world for pride, for pleasure, and for attack. The Holy Spirit sees the body and world as temporary devices for unlearning every concept in which the sleeping mind believes, emptying the mind of false belief, and making way for the Perspective which perceives a forgiven world.

In Awakening it becomes apparent that the ego had no unified goal or purpose. The ego was a mistaken identity. It sought to preserve itself, yet the "self" it perceived was ever changing, insecure, and had a deep sense of unworthiness.

With Awakening comes the awareness that Spirit is not the ego. The ego "self" was not real for it was not created by God and thus had no basis or foundation. The ego could have been described as the belief in death, for to believe that it was possible to make a self apart from the Self God created Perfect was to believe in death. The miracle shows that since the ego had no real effects it also had no existence. It takes faith in miracles to demonstrate the unreality of the ego and the world. Where the darkness seemed to be, there is now a miracle. And as you allow the miracle to radiate through you it becomes apparent that the dreamer of the dream is not at the mercy of the dream. It dawns in awareness that the purpose for the dream has changed from death to forgiveness. The Holy Spirit's Perspective now sees that all things work together for good, for that which is whole remains whole.

I have a transcribed dialogue in our Awakening Mind Online Library Publications that will be helpful in becoming clear about Purpose and choice. As you become clear about your Purpose, the actions and steps you are to take will simply follow and flow naturally.

In addition, Resta is sending you a set of CDs and one of the songs from Volume 4 is "What Is It For?" This song came after a kitchen table talk we had about the question "What is it for?" as applied to the same kinds of concepts you are currently pondering: relationships, occupation, personal goals, etc. You can listen to the song at our web site (see bibliography).

The next step is always obvious when it flows from a clear awareness of Purpose. Everything the Holy Spirit suggests flows from the Purpose of unified perception and seeing the tapestry of the cosmos as whole. This perception makes way for Divine Silence, and nothing is more "Productive" in the Truth than Divine Silence. Miracles will melt away your resistance to the Sweet Silence. :)

Blessings of Love & Joy Beloved One.

Love, David

NOBODY CAN TELL YOU
WHO YOU ARE

Dear David,

Thanks so much for your non-compromising introductory writings and willingness to help.

At the end of 1997 I had an experience in the presence of a Teacher of God who said he was leaving here and going home. In that moment all I heard was this was the last chance I had and I was terrified he'd "leave" without me. I then proceeded to stand still and entered into a point of grief so deep while holding onto the idea of God until every cell in my body opened up and the idea "I'm a martyr" was exposed and in the next instant I heard the voice say "You are my Son in Whom I am well pleased." The next thought that entered my mind was, "I need do nothing." In the next moment I found myself back in the room amongst these teachers of God. And I didn't know what was going on but I felt frightened. I really thought I'd just stand still and with all my desire to know God, I would be beyond perception forever and it would be "dream over." I was confused to find myself back in the room where I'd been standing prior to wanting above all else to give up the world. I went home, forgot about everything that had happened and peace came over me filling me with a joy I'd never experienced before. That night all the chapters of ACIM rolled through my mind like a current of light. And I woke up singing with joy.

I didn't really understand the importance of mind training and eventually I became very, very fearful and so guilty that I reached a point of depression and feeling imprisoned that I really didn't know was possible. Finally when I must have made the decision, I couldn't go on like this and used some worldly therapy to begin getting a little "currency" going activated again, I began applying the workbook and some other tools for forgiveness, and I began to have glimpses of peace and happiness and "seeing" the light behind the form, and feeling I was beginning to follow the Holy Spirit's guidance which was given specifically, and learning to trust. I was even beginning to wake up in the morning full of joy and singing as I awoke.

Then one day I was confronted by one of my teachers who vehemently declared that all I wanted was a boyfriend and I was so rebellious and defiant, that I would only remain as potential and never bear fruit. I was absolutely devastated and again experienced lots of mixed feelings of guilt and hopelessness and fear. I threw away all trust I'd had in myself and doubted then what seemed to be miraculous experiences that had been occurring.

Since that time I have been desperately applying the lessons in an attempt to forgive myself and those involved in the situation. Intellectually I can see there was none to blame. It was a mistake and in a sense my teacher was revealing the fear I'd held since that moment in 1997, that is – I really didn't have a sincere desire to learn and follow His direction and to know the Truth and that I wasn't really worth the effort. I've been experiencing a lot of rage and self-hatred, guilt and fear – even though I'm allowing the feelings to surface they just seem to shift around between fear guilt, anger, depression and loathing but I never really seem to release them. My mind feels strained with a big lump in it and I feel like I'm in a bit of a quandary. It's my decision to let this grievance go but it seems like I really want to hang onto it and justify my worthless, pathetic self-image in order to be right. I'm applying the work book lessons as best as I know how but nothing's budging. I might experience a couple of seconds of relief but that isn't the peace and joy and light of God that is really available to me to share with everything.

It just seems like I'm in complete rejection of the only thing that could truly help me and without a complete change of mind – 360-degree turn around, my learning is precarious if it can be threatened in any way yet it seems trust has to be developed. Any insights into how to move a stubborn mule? I kind of relate to the post "Nothing happening and not seeing." Feel like I'm full of crap and not releasing the core beliefs which are blocking my awareness to love's presence.

Thanks.

Beloved One,

Thanks for sharing your heart and your willingness to ask for Help. You have been Called to shine the Light as a teacher of God, a miracle worker. As you share the Light the Holy Spirit convinces the sleeping mind that it IS the Light. Nobody can tell you Who You are, yet the experience of Identity in God is inevitable. Do not look to man or woman for this recognition. There is nothing of the five senses that is reliable in recognizing the Truth of One Self. The Holy Spirit Guides unfailingly, and confidence will grow in accepting the Correction for all doubt and error. All doubt is doubt about Self.

When someone seems to tell you a lie about Self, the only response from the Spirit within is gentle laughter. "Choose again and you will see this differently" washes the mind free of doubt for a willing heart and thankful mind. Outgrow the concept of an "external" teacher, and see how quickly the confidence in miracles grows. Authentic Awakening rests on trust, honesty, and integrity and is a Living demonstration of Divine Love. Role models fall by the wayside as the Inner recognition dawns. Seek not outside our Self, for all idols have fallen away before the Light of our Eternal Love. You are the One! That is the Fact.

Love and Blessings Always, David

BRAIN/MIND CONFUSION

Dear David,

As a student of ACIM for almost a year, I have benefited greatly from its lessons and ideas. I remember reading that the brain of the human has nothing to do with the mind. Am I correct in this? As for my question, if I was hit by a truck and suffered brain damage, or had a major mental illness, or later suffered from organic brain syndrome, would I still have contact with universal mind (God)? I hope you don't find this too ignorant of a question and will offer a response as this has bothered me for some time...

I offer love/peace and forgiveness to all my brothers...

Beloved One,

Thanks for writing. Yes you are correct – the brain has nothing to do with Mind. The brain, like the body & earth & stars & cosmos, is a projection of the ego, or belief in separation. Everything of the cosmos was made to mimic or substitute for the Reality of Spirit. The brain was the ego's attempt at making up a mind. The brain is temporary. The Mind Eternal. The brain is an unreal effect of an unreal cause. The Mind is One with God, the Cause or Source of All. The brain follows instructions and does what it is told to do. The Mind is the residence of God, the Holy Spirit, and Christ.

All seeming sickness is the ego belief held in mind. The mind was sick that believed the brain could have a dysfunction. Mental illness is the belief that it is actually possible to sepa-rate from a Loving Creator. Mental illness is the belief that mind can be split into both love and fear. Therefore "brain damage" or "organic brain syndrome" are nothing more than ego attempts to project the "belief problem" to form by calling the "belief problem" a "brain problem."

"Brain damage" and "Organic brain syndrome" have no meaning to the Holy Spirit, Who looks not to effects. The Holy Spirit knows that they have no cause and therefore cannot be at all. As you work with the Holy Spirit and ACIM you will be carried to the forgiven world in the mind, and from this Perspective will perceive a reflection of Reality: a healed cosmos. The body is neutral and cannot be endowed with the characteristics of Spirit or ego. If you believe that the body can be sick, you are perceiving from a wrong-minded perspective and seem to have temporarily blocked your connection with the Universal Mind of God. The miracle shows the world to you anew, and in the miracle all seeming "suffering" has gone. In the right-mindedness of the miracle, suffering is impossible, for the miracle reflects the Light of the Holy Spirit Who is the Comforter and the Bridge to remembrance of God.

Before healing can be accepted in mind it is necessary to realize that the one problem is a perceptual problem. The problem is the lens that you were looking through, not the specifics that were perceived through the darkened lens of misperception. "Brain damage" and "Organic brain syndrome" are specifics without a cause because all misperceptions have no real cause. God is a real Cause and Christ and Creation proceed from a real Source. Atonement is seeing that this is a Fact and that nothing else exists. But first it is important to see that all sickness is mental sickness and has nothing to do with a brain.

The ego was made by belief and is dispelled as the mind ceases to believe in it. It is really this simple. If one scrap of false belief remains held in mind, the Truth of Divine Mind will seem obscured from awareness. Divine Mind simply Is and Is All that can be Known. I rejoice in your work with ACIM and the Holy Spirit. It will bring you lasting peace and joy and happiness!

Love & Blessings, David

Self Forgiveness

Dear David,

I have been one to always get enthused with truth teachings. I would read something inspiring and right away think so and so needs to hear this. They have a problem and this will help them. Now I know I did that with my ex-husband, and then I think about it now I am sure that's how I ended up divorced. I certainly wasn't seeing him perfect if I thought always there was something he needed to know. I still do this, I read something you write and ego says so and so needs to hear this and I send it. Usually there is no response. The old saying don't give advice unless asked, is what I am thinking lately. I am feeling now that these lessons are for self and shared only if asked. What are your thoughts on this?

One other question. I have numbness in my legs and have tried chiropractors and herbs, etc., everything but doctors. This has been for several years. Not constant but seems to be worse. I seem to be able to see people healed when I hear of their illness and they no longer seem to have what ails them. Is this harder to do for self? I read about there is no body, how do we release symptoms?

Thank you so much for being there. I don't know of anyone else to ask these types of questions.

Beloved One,

Thanks for your e-mail. As you are willing to be helpful and are open to having Help come through you it becomes apparent that whatever is shared is always one's own lesson. The Holy Spirit offers ideas that are helpful, and always gently reminds the mind: "It is your lesson." Miracles are involuntary, and if you find that you are trying to direct where they are offered, the ego is misdirecting the effort.

The Holy Spirit never seeks to fix or change anybody – only to Accept our brothers and sisters exactly as they are (Spirit). This is because mind is unified and every apparent brother and sister is the same opportunity to forgive the illusion and recognize the Self.

One is not a brother's keeper, one is unified in everything one perceives. As you see him you see yourself; as you treat him you treat yourself; as you think of him you think of yourself. This applies equally to the body you think of as your own. The ego mind tries to numb the pain of the belief in separation by projecting this numbness to the body. As you forgive the insane belief in separation from God, the body is used as a neutral instrument, for there is no attempt to project or reject or get rid of anything. Mind is healed as it accepts forgiveness and sees the impossibility of attack. Mind is unified and cannot attack or be attacked.

Remember this simple thought: I am not a body and my mind cannot attack, so I cannot be sick. All Glory to God for creating Spirit Eternal and One forever!!!

Love, David

THROUGH THE DARKNESS TO THE LIGHT

Hi David,

Well I must say I have been experiencing a lot of guilt and shame over the last week. Wow... in the center of that pain I applied all the concepts that I know... I can't remember ever feeling such pain. I know it's my attachment to the world.

Every day for the last week I felt like I was a dirty sinner. My guilt is growing... my feelings of unworthiness, and desirability. I know intellectually that it's not true, but I'm feeling it. Today was the day I just surrendered and began to feel and see the miracles. I was getting ready for night shift and I felt the peace and love. Then when I got on the bus this evening and a nice old lady looked and me and said, "I like it in the evening... it's romantic" I smiled. Then she looked at me and said "you're cute." I began to remember a talk you had about how you thought that Jesus thought everybody was cuties.

I began to feel love's presence and then two little girls walked on the bus with 'cute' on the front of their shirts. Then as I began to remember and feel loves' presence a lady got on the bus and sat next to me. The lady had a quilt and all over the quilt it said, "Jesus loves you... the bible says so." It said, "Heaven's gate within" and much more. Wow just the last few days I'd been feeling so alone and I was asking for his help. It's nice to have his love when in the darkest of times.

I love you David and will see you in a blink of an eye...

Beloved One,

Overflowing gratitude for your willingness to move through all of the emotions of darkness and inward to the Light. Thanks for your willingness to surrender to God's gentle Guidance within and release the past. Everyone is Called, though seemingly few choose to listen. Thanks for listening and following the Call of our Heart.

Peace is its own reward, Joy is natural, and Love is Who You are. I know You by your fruits and your sincerity. Thanks for showing up for God, and for your willingness to know the Self that God creates forever Perfect.

I Love You forever and ever! David

TRANSFER OF TRAINING MEANS MAKING NO EXCEPTIONS

Thanks again, David, for all your loving help. In this letter I'd like you to comment on my "style" of contemplation, so to speak, and then on a specific question about why the ego doesn't disappear as soon as the root belief behind its illusory appearance is exposed as impossible.

The way I contemplate or meditate has changed a lot since receiving your help. I start simply by saying, "Holy Spirit" and almost always the first thought is "rest in stillness and silence" or something similar. Then, a series of three things begin to happen, with pauses of silence in between:

1. I contemplate the holiness of "I", the "I" that is utterly uninvolved with my ego, the "I" that doesn't identify itself as "I am Ben" but as "I am I."

2. As I do this contemplation, it is periodically interrupted with the intrusion of an ego thought of some kind and when this happens I "Translate" the erroneous thought to the Truth the error was a lie about. This has so far been very easy and only takes a few seconds, after which I return to contemplating "I" in silence.

3. Anyway, it's occurred to me several times that truly egoless "I" is 100% ONE with the Trinity (which is also 100% ONE), and that there are as yet unknown or denied ego beliefs that are blocking my full experience of this. Now even though I'm quite happy to "Translate" these ego beliefs as they come up one by one during my contemplation, a few times I thought to myself, I'm just clipping off limbs from this tree (ego), let me Translate the root of the ego, and the whole tree will meet oblivion, including the unknown or denied "limbs" that are only part of the illusory appearance of the TREE, not part of the holiness of "I." Why should they continue to hang around when they've

just been proven to be nothing too? If I'm not mistaken, the root of the ego is the belief that separation from God is possible, immediately followed by the belief that separation from God has succeeded (in the form of ego). Well, this is very easy to Translate because it is absolutely clear that God is Truth and separation from Truth by definition would be a non-Truth and hence not exist, and I then and there decide to quit believing in the existence of something that doesn't exist.

Shouldn't the ego dissolve into the nothingness from whence it came at that point? Why doesn't the whole ego just disappear at that point?

Hello Beloved,

The ego does seem to dissolve or disappear when the temptation to project the belief in separation is no more. This is one's sole responsibility – to make absolutely no attempt to project responsibility for the ego and thus accept completely the Correction for the ego that the Holy Spirit offers. Your contemplation practice is aimed at just this. You are correct that your practice seems as if you are clipping off the limbs of the ego tree. This is how it will seem as long as there is a belief that the one error is many. To release the illusion of many is to see that there can never be a hierarchy of illusions, or preferences among illusions. Without a preference, the truth is revealed exactly as it is. And this experience has brought an end to all questions, for Certainty is far beyond a shadow of doubt.

Workbook Lesson 79 mirrors the idea that before the ego seems to disappear, the "problem" must be recognized exactly as it is (in mind) – not as it seems to be (specific in form). All spiritual practice aims at this one recognition, and linear time was made to deny this one simple recognition. Problems are not specific, though that is how they seem to the sleeping mind. The Correction sees that all the problems were the same, and thus are they gone all together. Be

grateful that you have given the mind permission to allow the "exceptions" it has attempted to begin to rise into awareness. Without protection you will see that they have gone, for they were all the same. Make no exceptions in your transfer of training, and you will see that truth has no exceptions.

Peace of mind is the proof that illusion has gone. Desire the experience wholly and the experience is holy. The practice or the seeking is actually the attempt to place the experience in the future. Yet the experience of Enlightenment is immediate. Anything which seems to deny this immediacy is but an opportunity for Atonement or complete forgiveness. Hope is potential. Enlightenment is Actual. Hope beckons a bright future. Enlightenment rests content in the Eternal Present. Hope offers anticipation. Enlightenment IS what Enlightenment offers.

I am joined with you in making no exceptions to the truth, for there are none. Love is without an opposite and Joy is unlimited Being. You are the One Beloved of God.
Rest in God's Peace.

Love, David

NOT USING MIRACLES AS
SPECTACLES TO INDUCE BELIEF

Hello David!

I have a few questions for you that are on my mind...

1) ACIM says as a Miracle Principle that "Miracles should not be used as spectacles to induce belief"

If this is true, then how would you define Jesus' miracles such as feeding the multitudes, raising the dead, etc.?

2) Wayne Dyer really speaks to my soul! I see him and ACIM in perfect alignment with their teachings. Do you see the same consistency in teachings between ACIM and Ernest Holmes? And ACIM and The Unity Church?

Thank you as always for your wonderful help in poking holes (miracles) in my clouds that are blocking the Sun. I also would like to share with you a verse I came up with:

DON'T SEE THE SUN SHINING, BE THE SUN SHINING!

In Love.

Beloved One,

Thanks for sharing your questions. Miracles are always only for the mind of the perceiver or dreamer (Mind is One) and what seems to occur in form is merely symbolic. Miracles are for the mind that has the ears to hear, so to speak, or the willingness and readiness to behold. Seeming changes in form reflect the shift in mind of the miracle-minded, and though some of these changes seem to transcend "known physical laws," in Reality there are no "known physical laws." The Law

of Love (Spirit) is the only Reality. Feeding the multitudes and raising the dead were symbols of the Divine Law of Love Which has no limit or lack. It is truly the beatitudes, or state of mind that demonstrates the miracle has come. It is this state of mind in which consistency is possible, and this is a characteristic of Awakening.

"Consistent form" is a contradiction in terms, although behavior can seem to become more "stable" for the miracle-minded. The easy way to remember that miracles are not intended to be used as spectacles to induce belief is to remember that miracles are the means of Awakening for a mind that already "believes" yet is also willing to go beyond belief and "Be Still and Know That I Am."

The teachings you mention are all very helpful stepping stones in Awakening to Oneness. The Holy Spirit will Guide you to discern the true from the false in all regards, and the deeper you seem to go you will seem to transcend all linear concepts and come to an experience that will end all doubting. The teachings you mention have Oneness as their main focus, yet there are subtleties of ego concepts that are transcended completely in Enlightenment.

Your inner work with the Holy Spirit will instruct you on your inward movement and Help you lay aside every linear (past-future) concept (such as balance and process and growth and personality). You are moving steadily inward to the experience of Atonement, Christ, and God's Love. Thanks for your devotion to Truth!

Love Eternally, David

Using the Holy Spirit
to Dissolve Questions and
Experience Certainty

David,

You mention that we need to question all assumption. What do we use in our questioning? To what do we compare our assumptions? Let me give you an example of how I think so you can show me where I need to work. I'm going to question my assumption that I can question my assumptions:

I "assume" that questioning my assumptions means that I should un-decide whether I'm right or wrong about an assumption, so I should just let it be either way. But since I can't assume that my assumptions are correct, I can't assume that questioning my assumptions means as much. Furthermore, since I can't assume that I know the difference between right and wrong, or even assume such a difference exists, I couldn't possibly judge the correctness of my assumptions.

So what am I supposed to do with this? Become a floater? Release myself from all assumption? To me that would mean disassociating from all opinions, which I can see follows the Course, but I would fail to be productive in my comfort zone: society. My reasoning for this is that due to my ego's love of logic, I won't have an answer for anything anyone asks me. I'd fail to be able to provide for myself or others, monetarily speaking. I'd reply to questions like "How are you considering paying back your credit card debt?" with answers like, "Oh, I have a debt?" Soon I'd be pushed out of that comfort zone and have to become a hermit. Then the question becomes, is this the kind of behavior that will ultimately free my mind, or am I failing to listen to what you're saying but using my ego to interpret it?

Thanks for helping me out-the true me, whoever that is. I assume it's my ego that wants to be "enlightened," that my ego wants to pursue this because it's a nice diversion from God's plan. Its own logic would tell me that enlightenment is ego suicide, but since it represents an accomplishment over other people on this planet who don't appear to be enlightened, it keeps going.

Beloved One,

Thanks for your probing inquiry. It is only helpful to use the Holy Spirit for unveiling, exposing, and releasing assumptions. The Holy Spirit will reveal the impossibility of comparison or judgment entirely, and this is the Atonement. As one seems to train the mind (in a time process) with the Holy Spirit, the Holy Spirit will seem to judge, Guiding one very directly (with prompts and instructions) as long as one believes in specifics and situations. Your feelings are the one right use of judgment in the Awakening, and feelings of peace and joy and happiness are the barometer that lets you know you are following Divine Guidance.

The ego is the questioning aspect of the mind, but initially aiming these questions at assumptions or beliefs instead of at the projected cosmos is a helpful way of dissolving the questions. Let the Holy Spirit inspire your questions. As the ego assumptions dissolve, everything flows smoothly in mind and it begins to dawn that there is no objective world apart from the mind. The ego world was subjective and based on the assumptions held in mind. Beneath all opinions and conclusions and assumptions and beliefs is the truly productive State of Mind: the Divine Silence of Being. This productivity is Creation, the State of Spirit extending forever and ever. This productivity has nothing to do with the ego construct of "society."

The approach toward remembering Divine Creation includes yielding into, or surrender into, Divine Providence; seeing that every symbol is offered freely of the Holy Spirit. It does entail the thought about literally being unable "...to provide for myself or others, monetarily speaking." It places all trust in the Holy Spirit for supplying every seeming need, such as air, food, water, shelter, transportation, words, communication devices, etc. This does not necessarily mean you will identify yourself as a "hermit" but it does mean you will recognize that you are Divinely provided for in all seeming circumstances.

This thinking with the Holy Spirit will ultimately free the mind of its imaginary imprisonment. Behavior but flows from thought as thought flows from belief, so it is with belief and thought that the Holy Spirit works. You might think of behavior as a byproduct of thought, and that is why Correction is never at the seeming level of form. Think with God and be Happy is the aim of your work with the Holy Spirit. Christ is an Idea in the Mind of God. In following the Holy Spirit you will gain Certainty by aligning with the Holy Spirit's Purpose and making no exceptions or assumptions. Enlightenment is the awareness that only Love is real. Christ is Certain of Identity in God because Christ is the Child of God's Identity. All Glory to the One Spirit!

Love & Joy, David

SOME FUNDAMENTAL QUESTIONS

Dear Holy Brother,

I have read A Course in Miracles (ACIM) and reviewed both websites of "Foundation for ACIM" and "Awakening Mind." First, I would like to share with you, Holy Brother, how ACIM and your websites have helped me. It appears that ACIM was designed to transform one's mind, albeit awaken so that one is aware of the "ego" or "wrong mindedness." I also understand that I am the Son of God, my Mind is the Mind of God (and you are also the "Sons of God" as well Holy Brothers). I understand that everything outside of me (us) that I (we) see is a projection of what is in my (our) minds. But it was a projection of our guilt onto others, which is how the seemingly vast world and cosmos was made.

Yet, according to ACIM and the Truth, the vast world or cosmos that appears before us (based on using the body's five senses) is all false. Reason tells us that the splitting of our minds never happened. That is why, in Truth, I (we) have never "departed" from God. It is impossible to "depart" from God (or vice versa – that God departed from us). God is Whole. There is no possible escape from that God, whole and complete, because God just Is. Therefore, I am not the body. I am the Son of God. I am the Mind of God. I am the Spirit.

Jesus wanted to teach us to become aware of our mistake, that we chose the ego instead of the Holy Spirit while we "fell asleep" "mindless," so that we can be "awakened" "mindful" with the Mind of God. Once awakened, the ego disappears. Indeed, this appears to be a "process" like peeling off the layers of an onion or petals of a flower until there is nothing left (as the ego is nothing).

I understand the above and have no doubts at all. In fact, it is very practical to be "aware" or "mindful" (meaning to look within) at times. I am also aware that the ego world does not seem to dissolve, which tells me that what is within in my mind has not changed. This means that the problem (guilt) remains within my mind.

If I am not the body and everything around me, based on my five senses, is all false, then, why can't I simply "commit suicide" and then, instantly, I am back with God. This is silly because I understand that if I do not have a body, then, what is there to "kill" or commit suicide. Nothing! (Laughter) What I am trying to say is that I want to let go of the ego nonsense. Yet, if the ego nonsense is unreal or never existed, how can I let go of the "unreal" that never existed? Silly!

There has got to be a way (I know the quote from the Bible that Jesus is "The Way") to dissolve the seemingly unreal stuff instantly since there is no time (time does not exist in God) instead of a "process" (which by the way is making the time real). Please share your guidance.

In the New Testament, concerning the Resurrection, it said that Jesus reappeared to the Apostles (thus demonstrating "Resurrection" or death does not exist in the Son of God). This would also indicate (or be interpreted) that there is "life after death." It did not seem to share the idea or teaching of what happens when the ego is dissolved (the seeming false form of body is "dead"). Please share your guidance.

Finally, with respect to miracles, do miracles appear to our senses in response to the change (or "correction") in our Mind which is ultimately correcting the projection/perception? I understand that all worldly problems are seemingly different through our five senses, yet it is only one problem? If so, how can I change the mind (from "wrong mind" to "right mind") when there is no wrong mind in the first place? What I am trying to say is that, if there is no "wrong mind" or the ego world is false or I never "departed from God," why does the ego appear at all? If God never sleeps (the Spirit never sleeps – "sleep" does not even exist), then, the Son of God would never sleep as well, but in the Genesis or ACIM still mentions that I/we "fell asleep" and choose the "wrong mind" (dream world). How did that happen? What is the real Truth about that notion? Please share you guidance. Thank you Holy Brother.

With Love always.

Greetings Beloved One,

Thanks for your thoughtful questions and for your willingness to look within and be free of the ego illusion forever. I have answered your questions in depth on the Awakening In Christ Yahoo Group (see bibliography). You can use the "Search Archive" box near the bottom of the web site to zero in on the written answers to your questions and, more importantly, to the experiential Answer Within that ends all questions (Being Absolute Certainty).

ACIM points to an experience of the Present Moment, yet the experience of the Present Moment is beyond words (which are only symbols of symbols twice removed from Reality). My writings do the same. For the mind that desires Awakening, these answers and instructions are a Course in the Simple and the Obvious. Yet if the mind desires the illusion of separation, the Course will seem difficult and frustrating to apply. Desire is the Key to forgiveness of illusions. Truth will be returned to your awareness by your desire, as it was lost in awareness by your desire for something else. "Let thine eye be single" is a way of saying "Desire only Truth and you shall experience the Truth that has no opposite."

Desire healing wholly, and you are healed. For the Holy Spirit knows that the separation never happened, and offers this Correction, or Atonement, this very instant. You are correct in stating that "process" is a way of making time real. Yet to a mind that still believes in time, "process" is a gentle metaphor for allowing the seeming willingness for Awakening to grow stronger - so that Unified or Single Desire can be grasped without a fear of loss or sacrifice. Atonement

must be accepted voluntarily, and thus the sleeping mind is not "hurled into Reality." The mind must desire to Awaken, for the Holy Spirit does not command or demand or coerce. Though Awakening is inevitable and requires only One Instant of complete forgiveness, Awakening is never forced on the sleeping mind that dreams of exile from God. Miracles open the way to accepting the Correction (Atonement) without fear. For in Truth there is nothing to fear.

I was recently asked: "What is your belief in death? Do you believe in heaven and hell? Do you believe in reincarnation? Thank you for your help." My answer to these questions is always the same and I share it now as a basis for the more subtle questions you have asked. Under the instructions and direction of Jesus Christ I have been shown and experienced that there is no death for the Spirit I Am. This world was the belief in hell, yet through forgiveness I experience Heaven as Now and see that hell was but an error, an illusion that the Holy Spirit Corrected instantly. I live in the Joy of Christ and happily shine the Light in which I am created by our Loving God. "The Kingdom of Heaven is at hand" means it is Now, a state of Mind that is Innocent, untouched by the error that was sin (separation from God). I invite you to a journey of Awakening to the Christ Idea that resides forever in the Mind of God. Love is real. Hell and death were the illusions. Reincarnation is a stepping stone belief to Enlightenment or Salvation. Eternity is timeless, while reincarnation is a seeming story of the "soul" and "time." Unconscious beliefs in error and time must be questioned, forgiven and released, and you will happily see that they had no reality. Eternal Love is Reality, for God is Love and Christ is Love.

You stated: "I want to let go of the ego nonsense." I suggest doing the ACIM Workbook. Do it with such passion and desire that for each seeming lesson that you read you EXPECT to Awaken instantly. This suggestion is truly only a prayer for Unified Desire, and Unified Desire is Creation. The Holy Instant is the gateway to Creation, and the Workbook lessons were designed only as a reflection of the Purpose of Awakening and willingness to Awaken. If you apply your mind effort and willingness and try to not make exceptions to the lesson idea offered, the Holy Spirit will Guide the mind unfailingly into the awareness of the Holy Instant.

Resurrection is of the mind and for the mind, and the symbol of a resurrected body was meant only to point to a Resurrected mind (in which the ego has dissolved away). The body is a neutral symbol and truly neither lives or dies, so a "resurrected body" in this sense is a contradiction in terms. The symbol of the "resurrection" 2000 years ago was to teach that you cannot kill the Son of God, for Spirit cannot die (Being Eternal). One reaches awareness of Heaven through resurrection, or "healing of mind" by accepting Atonement or complete forgiveness. This comes by first allowing the Holy Spirit to discern between right and wrong-minded thinking and next by accepting only right-minded thinking or the forgiven world.

You asked: "...do miracles appear to our senses in response to the change (or 'correction') in our Mind which is ultimately correcting the projection/perception? I understand that all worldly problems are seemingly different through our five senses, yet it is only one problem? If so, how can I change the mind (from 'wrong mind' to 'right mind') when there is no wrong mind in the first place?" In Awakening it is important to keep the horse in front of the cart and not assume that the cart can pull the horse. Miracles and right-mindedness are the same, and this is simply seeing the false as false. Miracles and right-mindedness are the awareness that there is no causation in form and that the cosmos has not left the mind of the dreamer. If one seems to perceive separate persons, places, things, and situations, one believes in the illusion of wrong-mindedness.

The Holy Spirit sees the tapestry of the cosmos as one illusion, the false as false, and sees that there is nothing "outside" the Mind. There is only wholeness in this "Above the Battleground" Perspective. This unified Perspective is the same as right-mindedness, or the forgiven world. The change of mind of which you speak is accepting the mind's Changelessness and Singularity. The "how" is the Holy Spirit. Let the Holy Spirit decide for God for you, and you accept Atonement or "change your mind about your mind." Your part is only willingness, for the Might of the Holy Spirit joins with this little willingness to see the world anew. Say and mean: "Above all else I want to see this differently."

I have spoken often about the question: "How could the impossible happen?" There are many writings and tapes and CDs which address this question (the most asked question), though it must become apparent that you BELIEVE that the separation HAS happened if you watch your emotional state of mind. The assumption beneath the question is that the separation has ACTUALLY happened, and this is the belief or assumption (the ego) to question. Actually all questions arise from this belief or assumption (the ego), for the ego seemed to ask the "first question": "What am I?" Every subsequent question implies an identity confusion and is thus a denial of Identity as Christ. The experience of Awakening is the recognition of Self as Christ, and in this Certainty there is no such thing as a question. Oneness or Love has no opposite. Heaven is a State of Being, Pure Is-ness, Eternally. All seeming questions have time-space, private minds, and private thoughts as their basis. Yet Love knows Love, and Love is All there Is. Open to the experience of Love, and nothing "else" remains.

Love & Eternal Blessings, David

WHAT ABOUT THE HOLOCAUST?

David,

I have got a big question. When we use course principles, and please correct me if I am wrong, we say that what hurt us in the past never happened. What exactly does that mean?? For example if the course is saying that the Holocaust never happened, this is shocking and can be used by certain groups to justify anti-Jewish feelings. Can you help me to understand

Beloved One,

Thanks for your question. Miracles collapse time and offer a Correction for all misperception. As I shared in the earlier message about the concept of abuse, the ego is the belief that it is possible to be unfairly treated. It matters not whether the error of abuse seemed to take the form of mild annoyance or mass murder, for there are not different forms of the same illusion. Forgiveness lets go of all illusions together, and in forgiveness Innocence is recognized. Forgiveness is always a gift to One Self, for only the error of attack seemed to veil the Love within. The Spirit teaches that pardon is always justified, and peace and understanding go together. Pardon what never happened and accept that *What Is* is the pathway to the Happiness of Being Present.

The ego may seem to quote scripture and justify an "anti" feeling or opinion, yet the ego has no seeming existence, or power, or life, unless it is believed. It is helpful to question the unconscious ego belief system in abuse and victimhood, for once it is exposed as false it disappears from awareness. I am joined with you in forgiveness, and complete forgiveness is the awareness that the separation from God never happened. Indeed, only forgiveness is a worthy goal for your time and effort, for forgiveness yields peace of mind. Nothing can prevail against a Child of God Who knows of God's Eternal Peace.

Blessings Be Upon You Holy One. Love, David

What I Can Control vs.
what I Can't Control

Hi David,

Maybe you can help me to learn what I can control vs. what I can't control. I listened to your tape "No Control over the world" and found that it raised lots of confusion in my mind. I attach a file with my more detailed request for clarification.

When I was young, I thought I had control over everything in my life (work, who my friends were, what I did for pleasure and time off, what I did for hobbies, etc.). I thought I had no control over sickness, violence from others, war, accidents, etc. Now that I'm getting older (I'm fifty two) I need to wear glasses and find I can't see with them, or without them, my memory is failing, my ability to learn new technologies is getting more difficult, etc.

I find that I have less and less control over the loss of function, and that I'm heading to where my mother is, in a wheelchair, in a home. I seem to be at a loss to control the human decline. If I understand the tape, I might as well accept the fact that the body is aging and function is leaving. The mind would be at least relieved of the worry. It too is not as sharp as it was. I can't remember people's names and often words I know simply do not come, or come in the wrong language.

Anyway, I'm sure that your words of wisdom will shed clarity on these issues, so this is lesson 1 of "How to recognize what I can control vs. what I cannot control."

Love

Beloved One,

Thanks for writing and sharing your questions and ponderings. Awakening is simply the clear awareness that State of Mind (Peace, Happiness, Freedom, Joy) is true Self Responsibility and the belief (ego) that seemed to make the cosmos has had no effect on Reality (Truth of Spirit).

To live in the Present is to Be, free of the illusory limits of time-space. You can control the direction of your thinking and can therefore align with the Holy Spirit in the Present Moment. Practicing with willingness the ability to choose the Holy Spirit will yield the experience of Being, Which is far beyond the illusory concept of choice.

It is true that nothing is random. The script of the cosmos played out in one seeming "unholy instant" and was Corrected or Neutralized by the Holy Spirit. Flow with the Love of the Holy Spirit and it becomes apparent that all seeming decisions in form are already made. This is the experience of the happy dream of non-judgment. Prayer, mind watching, and forgiveness yield the experience that all form is false appearance and past, and what is past cannot be changed – only recognized as over and gone. Time and space are one illusion, and peace of mind comes the Instant the illusion is forgiven or released.

Life is our Spirit, Which is Eternal. The body only seems to decline and age to the ego; the belief in time. Be comforted to know that Holy Spirit will arrange time and space for the miracles you will be sharing. Our joining shows that time has had no effect on our Identity in God. Nothing can change Eternal Love. What seems to fade was never Love, for Love is Everlasting.

Continue to open to the miracles the Holy Spirit offers. Listen to the gatherings offered online, pray for the Holy Spirit's Loving Interpretation, and everything will be revealed. Awakening is a Moment of readiness and willingness, and actually has nothing to do with time at all. Give your mind permission to rest and soar in the Divinity within. Miracles offer an effortless way of flowing in the Moment, and you will recognize them by the Ease through which they come. Release all attempts to control persons, places, and events, and watch with the Holy Spirit. Keep watch and there is only an experience of light-heartedness. Nothing else really matters.

Love & Blessings Now & Always, David

WHAT IS ABSTRACT LIGHT?

Dear David,

I am confused when I hear you use the term "Abstract Light." In my understanding, it is the words and concepts which are the abstractions (detachment or "drawing away"). God then would be the only truly concrete (or non-abstract) thing which exists.

I have considered that perhaps you are saying that God is not really "light" in the worldly sense (photons), but that light happens to be a good symbol for God, and therefore the concept is used as an abstraction for God. If that is what you mean, why IS light a good symbol? Is it because light symbolizes truth (illumination) and the blessings of sunshine? I certainly don't mean to reduce God to word play. It is only that I have been confused about this matter for some time. I had been under the impression that ACIM really was referring to light as photons. This certainly intrigued me, but left me deeply baffled. :)

Hello Beloved One,

Thanks for writing. Abstract Light has no form or matter to it, and is not concrete or specific in any way. Abstract Light is the Light of Understanding. Abstraction is the natural condition of the Mind; formless Abstraction. God knows not form. You might think of this Light as the Light mentioned in many "near death" accounts. The cosmos is a cosmos of time-space, many seeming concrete specifics, degrees, intervals, levels, increments, etc. Abstraction is beyond this, for before time-space was, I Am. I Am is Pure Abstraction. There is nothing of this world which has any relation to Divine Abstraction.

Blessings of Love, David

What is Real?

David,

Are you real? Or are you just part of the dream, representing my desire to awaken. Am I the only being in the world? There is no Peace House, is there? Unless of course I decided to go there, then it would all be exactly as I made it up to be. There never really was a man named Jesus. This is all contrived. I made you up, didn't I?

Beloved One,

I am real. There is only One. You are the One. I am the One. There is no David in Reality, yet David can be used by the Holy Spirit as a symbol or reflection of the desire to Awaken. There is no you in Reality, yet you can be used by the Holy Spirit as a symbol or reflection of the desire to Awaken. The same applies to Jesus. There is only the Spirit that God created Eternal. There is no Peace House in Reality, and yes if you seemed to decide to go "there" it would be exactly as the ego made it up to be. Perception is selective and subjective through the ego's lens, and there is no objective world apart from the perceiver. The ego made the cosmos, yet the Holy Spirit uses what the ego made to lead to the Kingdom of Heaven within. Love is All there Is. Eternity Shines!

Love, Oneness

WHEN WILL THIS THIRST END?

Dear Davidji,

Lots of miracles keep occurring. Often sometimes more than often, the awareness of the Truth "hits" one. But yet there are times like this morning when one gets bogged down by others' reactions to these miracles. One's thoughts then go wandering into territory which one "knows" is not real. This morning one was besieged by these thoughts. One lay down, contemplated on the Self, prayed, called on the Holy Spirit, said one's mantras, and the "fight" seemed endless. There was hollow in the pit of the stomach. All along one was fully aware that one's mind was in the "wrong" place. Yet whatever one did seemed to be useless.

This barrage of thoughts just kept coming. Now several hours later some easiness has set in. But still one feels that this is not enough. There is more to be felt and be... why is this avoiding one when one wants it so badly? How to? Deep hunger still prevails and there is a gnawing at the Heart. When will this thirst end?

Love as always.

Beloved One,

Thanks for pouring out your heart and for your devotion to Awakening. The thirst for the remembrance of Self and God is what seems to propel the search, the quest. It is the Call to remember What is Forever True. The thirst ends in the experience of the Answer within, and this is experienced as it is obvious there is nothing of this world to hold on to or desire.

Nothing.
No thing.
No concept.
No belief.
No want.
No need.
No time.

Truth is approached through negation. Look directly at everything that Truth is not, "others' reactions" "thoughts" and what remains constant is the Truth that Is.

The invulnerability of Christ rests in the willingness to align only with Real thoughts and the Holy Spirit's Perspective. What seems to be "others' reactions" are doubt thoughts which seem to veil the Face of Christ. You are the One. Mind is One. There can be no "self" and "other" in a mind unified through forgiveness. Mind is unified and cannot meaningfully be broken into separate parts. Surrender is the Answer. It is impossible to let go of "something" that was never there. Now is All.

Love, David

FAITH OR WORKS?

Hi David,

Just a few lines regarding some discussion in our midst I thought you might like to comment on when you get some time.

The discussion seems to come down to the age old controversy in Christendom; Works or Faith. On the one hand one can believe that the Course is a process that ends in the Holy Instant. And that the process is [works] – removing all the obstacles to peace until the Holy Instant is realized. While the other is [faith] believing that the Holy Instant is NOW, in the present moment. And that thought is held in the mind by the power of the Holy Spirit, a choice made by the decision maker – made by I – (You, the Son of God). One can believe, this moment, that he is either a miserable sinner, "the home of evil darkness and sin" or the free Son of God.

The whole ACIM Chapter 15 is very interesting in this regard and I quote two passages to make my point.

ACIM (T.15 I.10) "Time is inconceivable without change, yet holiness does not change. Learn from this instant more than merely that hell does not exist. In this redeeming instant lies Heaven. And Heaven will not change, for the birth into the holy present is salvation from change. Change is an illusion, taught by those who cannot see themselves as guiltless. There is no change in Heaven because there is no change in God. In the holy instant, in which you see yourself as bright with freedom, you will remember God. For remembering Him is to remember freedom."

(T.15 I.11) "If you are tempted to be dispirited by thinking how long it would take to change your mind so completely, ask yourself, "How long is an instant?" Could you not give so short a time to the Holy Spirit for your salvation? He asks no more, for He has no need of more. It takes far longer to teach you to be willing to give Him this than for Him to use this tiny instant to offer you the whole of Heaven. In exchange for this instant He stands ready to give you the remembrance of eternity."

Therefore, it comes down to a question of belief. Does it not? Paul in his letter to the Galatians Ch 3 opens out this dichotomy in another way. "Oh! Foolish Galatians! Who has bewitched you that you should not obey the truth ...did you receive the Holy Spirit by the works of the law or by the hearing of faith?" Paul believed that his faith made him guiltless and free from sin!

The little book "The Cloud of Unknowing" states that God is held by the heart and not the intellect. "By love can he be caught and held, but by thinking never."

There seems to be a view that the Course is heavy on process and light on faith. I would hope you can discuss this and expand on it.

Peace, joy and love.

Greetings Beloved One,

Thanks for your subtle question. You wrote: "Therefore, it comes down to a question of belief. Does it not?" Atonement is a belief that takes One Instant to accept, and therefore Atonement is not a matter of time. Atonement seems to take the form of "a decision to accept Correction" for a mind that believes in opposites and choice. The belief in linear time is the ego, as is the belief in a "decision-maker." The Holy Spirit IS the "final" decision that is inevitable. A Course In Miracles contains words which are used by the Holy Spirit to speak to the mind which believes it is an ego and has separated from God.

The seeming "process" of Awakening is the illusion of "giving up" the ego, and therefore the "works" that are inspired by the Holy Spirit during the "process" of Awakening are illusion as well. Let the seeming "Works" be inspired

and Guided by the Holy Spirit and the seeming results are "more and more" sustained experiences of love, peace, happiness, joy, and freedom in awareness.

In Perfect "Faith" there is the Perception of Wholeness. In this Perspective there are no longer separate "Works," just one beautiful Tapestry. This beautiful Tapestry quickly gives way to the Instant of Revelation, the Holy Instant, which is the Pure Light of God. Desire the Holy Instant, for It cannot be denied in Truth. Forget this world, forget this Course, and come with wholly empty hands unto your God. This is a Call to remember the Holy Instant. This is truly the Aim of A Course In Miracles and Self-realization. Wholeness knows Wholeness, and there are no parts. Faith knows Faith, and there are no works. Love knows Love, and there is nothing else.

In Loving Kindness, David

TAKE THE LEAP OF FAITH

Hi David,

I have been on your list for a month or two. I have been reading ACIM on and off since 1995, but it's only two months ago that I started to put the lessons and reading text into a daily routine, mostly out of desperation.

Now the main reason I am writing you is from what I can tell by your responses to people on the list, you seem to have a real handle on the principles of ACIM, like you are really, truly living it. What was your life like before ACIM, and how is it different now? Was there some negative circumstance that brought you to ACIM first?

I have been long battling severe anxiety and depression. I am now 33, and at a big crossroads in my life. I know positive change is coming soon, yet a lot of times I don't trust that things will ever get better. I feel like I have been suffering forever, and so much of the time I am filled with frustration and hatred for myself for my negative, fearful thinking which seems to plague me. My investment in ego thinking is so strong I fear I will never recover my true self.

I am a singer & songwriter, and career issues have been tied up with my identity for a long time. I left a good job a year ago to pursue the music, but once again, my anxiety & depression took over and I just can't seem to move forward and have enough confidence in myself to face the world and share my talent. I am afraid of my own power and the attention I would get from people because of this talent. My ego wants it, but also makes me terrified of it.

I have been unemployed all this time and I am racking up thousands of dollars in credit card debt. In a few months my cash reserves will be gone. It seems that that's what it will take to get me moving out of my apartment into the world or to pick up a phone and start making connections. I am afraid of people basically. I am afraid of rejection, failure and success, both in my career as a musician, and in social/romantic relationships. I have very low self-esteem, even though I have everything in the world going for me that most people would give anything to have.

I don't know what to do for myself anymore. I've tried therapy, self-help books, everything. I do believe my only answers at this point lie in the Course. But even through my study of it I cannot seem to completely let the ego go. I have too much time and energy invested into it. It would feel like I was losing myself if I completely let it go. There are days where I have noticed improvement, but when I go down, I really go down. I really don't know how to help myself anymore, because I feel like my own worst enemy. I have felt like something is "wrong" with me since childhood. I don't know what to do. I don't know how to study the Course every day and still on some level be resisting its teachings. Marianne Williamson answered a question of mine during her web cast, and she said "it would take a miracle" for me to make this transition and finally take the leap of faith.

But what does that mean? Do I just keep studying the Course and hope that someday it will work on me? Or is there something more I need to do? Psychologists would tell me there is no answer except to take action. (God helps those who help themselves.) But I am an avoidance addict. I am afraid to take action. I am afraid to reach out to people. The longer I live in isolation, the harder it gets. I just don't know what to do. I feel like I am really missing the boat here, just not getting it. Any insights you could offer me would be greatly appreciated.

Thank you.

Beloved One,

Thanks for pouring your heart out and sharing your thoughts; for not protecting them is a big step toward healed

perception. The willingness to ask for Help is a reflection of the desire for healing. I came to the Inner Voice for God long before ACIM came into my awareness, and now I experience Life as Oneness with God and All. The Principle of Love is Alive Now as a State of Being! Initially the Holy Spirit used the contrast between fear and love as a way of showing that there must be a better way than the past seemed to offer. As the willingness to follow as Guided seemed to grow in strength, the happy lessons of forgiveness followed and linked in a circle of Atonement. In Atonement Now I am aware that the separation and the story never happened. Love simply Is.

First it is important to be open to the idea that it is impossible not to know God's Will for Perfect Happiness. Hesitation offers nothing. Delay is futile. Love is inevitable. You have gifts to give over to the Holy Spirit to use for Awakening. It will increasingly seem more and more impossible not to use these talents for the Glory of God. Anything that does not Glorify the Creator is a wisp of illusion that will pass away from awareness.

Open your heart to allow the Holy Spirit to make contacts for you and bring holy witnesses into your awareness. The backdrop will be a scenario for allowing the Holy Spirit to initially take care of credit card debts for you, and for you the path will be rich with holy encounters and opportunities to brighten your attitude. Simplify your world as a reflection of the desire to simplify your thoughts and align with the Holy Spirit. Take time to read and practice ACIM and do the Workbook lessons. Let it be a path of devotion. Use the free resources on our web site and feel free to attend a gathering or reach out to those that are Awakening along with you. You are not alone, for God goes with you everywhere you seem to go. The Presence of God is unmistakable for a willing mind and thankful heart.

The illusion of isolation will begin to fade in awareness as you trust the Holy Spirit with each small step you take. You have taken a big step by writing this e-mail. Your seeming "problem" is not private anymore, for you have opened it up to the Holy Spirit.

All of the legions of angels await your tiny nod of willingness to spring into action on your behalf. Jump in, for Love is the "safety net" underneath the seeming leap, and the Holy Spirit will surely carry you through the darkness to the Light! No one can fail who seeks to reach the Truth. I am with You Holy One of God.

Blessings raining down, David

SEARCHING FOR A CALLING

David,

I have spent the last year in turmoil of losing a house, giving up belongings, a garden and pool, lots of space to smaller space; then moving alone. I have been searching for a calling, the path where I am to go to be used in the Spirit. It seems as if it is holding out for something as I am still waiting for direction.

Patiently Aging.

Beloved One,

Thanks for writing. Yes, the Holy Spirit is Calling. Everyone is Called, though in this world few seem to listen to or answer the Call. Yet nothing of the world matters to Eternity. Peace and Happiness are a matter of decision and the willingness to decide for God. The Call can seem to get covered over with many distractions and ego pursuits, yet the Call remains. The Call, if followed, will Guide one toward the Holy Instant in which Love simply Is. Everything I share is Given freely as assistance in answering the Call. With a little willingness the door to the turnaround will be apparent. Make use of all that is offered. Take the baby steps of 'a little willingness', and above all expect miracles, for they are natural and a reflection of our Heavenly Inheritance. Use the many resources that are offered on our web site as a beginning. I am with You all the way! I Love You dearly.

Love always, David

WHAT IS LIFE
WITHOUT GOALS AND AMBITIONS?

David,

What is life without goals and ambitions? I mean I have heard so many times people quoting "Man without a dream or a vision shall perish." Aim or a goal in life drives us to do work or action and that keeps us busy and occupied. Now even if we try to do action just for the sake of action and not for any rewards or fulfillment of desires, still how do we pick any action without a purpose? I mean I brush my teeth to keep them clean and it is a hygienic thing to do.

If you say you reply to people's emails and do talks I am sure there is a goal, aim or purpose behind it. You would like to help people. But again choosing you as an example would not be the right thing to do as you are an exception! So many people, people with good intentions, people seeking peace of mind, you know the majority of them do action driven by an aim or goal. Goal being "where do I see myself 5 years from now if I do what I choose to do now?" "What should I do today that takes care of my family now and also in the future," and so on and so forth?

Goal, ambition or aim is a thing of the future. So I guess my question again is what is living in the present if the essence of the "present" is the past and the future, I mean present does not exist without a past or future.

Hello Beloved One,

Thanks for your sincere question. It seems that life is moving forward in this world, and that time and progress move forward toward the future. Future goals seem to aim at something better than the past or present. Yet the past is gone

and the future is but imagined. Both are defenses against the Present Moment and the realization that everything is Perfect right Now.

In Awakening time seems to collapse, it seems to shorten, and it seems to move backward toward the original error and then disappear entirely in the Innocence that precedes the error. In Awakening time is like a carpet that rolls back and rolls up completely, so that nothing is left at all. The Present is before time was. This is another way of saying what Jesus taught: "Before Abraham was, I am."

Awakening is remembering Original Innocence, and this Enlightenment experience has everything to do with Now and nothing to do with time. The essence of the Present Moment is Eternity, and Now has nothing to do with linear time, or past, or future. Life is a State of Mind. With regard to this world, the closest approximation of Eternity is Now. Now is the rebirth of Spirit in awareness. Now is free of past regrets and grievances and future worries and anxious plans. There is a meaning to the quote you share, "Man without a dream or a vision shall perish." Without the happy dream of non-judgment, without the Vision of Christ, everything of this world does seem to perish, for nothing of this world is Everlasting.

Goals and ambitions seem practical in the world, yet if they are aimed at the future and future outcomes I assure you that they are ego motivations. Present Peace is a "goal" worth desiring, for it is more than possible, it is inevitable. The experience of Present Peace results from listening only to the Spirit within, and to the Spirit there is no tomorrow. The Holy Spirit uses time to teach that there is no time. This is the Purpose that inspires and blesses and even seems to motivate action until the awareness dawns that nothing is really happening. The happy dream is like a lucid dream in which the dreamer is aware of dreaming. Dreams are not taken to be Reality, and sleep is not taken to be Wakefulness.

If you feel like you are driven to "do things," ask yourself if there is a fear of consequences. If you believe that to not "do things" will result in fearful consequences, then it is wise to examine what is believed. As long as fearful beliefs are held as true, thoughts and actions will be fear-driven. Forgiveness is a miracle and it releases the mind from fear of consequences. Let the Holy Spirit be the Purpose that gently Guides, and you will never feel "driven" again! Value not one belief the ego sponsors and enjoy the experience of Divine Ease. Not one seeming difficulty but will melt away before you reach it.

Accept Present Bliss as our Purpose, and watch how bright the world seems in awareness. Seek not to change the world, seek rather to change your mind about the world. Enlightenment is as simple as accepting the Changeless as True. For there is nothing else but Love! All Glory to God!

Love Everlasting, David

FURTHER CLARIFICATION
ABOUT AWAKENING

Dear David,

I am writing again as I am in need of further clarification of what is really happening. I am sober now nine years. I am very aware of the awakening process that began at that time and now it's taken on a very different feel. Since beginning ACIM and becoming dedicated to the Truth, I have had so many of my ego thoughts just disappear. And it's very unsettling because they are attached to bodies and it's just weird. I may sound crazy and I feel that way a lot, but the speed at which they are dissolving is indeed mind boggling. I know that my favorite projection is guilt. I have had so much to release and yet the people in my life that I thought were pure and innocent all have had recent happenings which forced me to find the innocence. I know that my thoughts are being purified and ideas don't leave their source, so all is within me, my own judgments are being seen, it's almost like my whole life is being replayed and allowing me to get it right!

I really don't think I'm making sense here after reading this. But I will go on. I thought that getting sober would be about being able to "participate in the world." To be a part of, to be of service to others and of course to support myself. I have been able to do that but at what cost? I am tired all the time, I do things I don't want to do and yet I'm still afraid to do nothing. To just be. I choose this job that I'm at right now and I accept that. I don't want to move farther away from the Truth, yet I don't want to stay at this job much longer. I am afraid that if I leave, "others" will say, I'm forever running, never satisfied, always moving from one job to the other, can't count on me to stay put, I'm leaving a secure position, benefits; I am walking away from insurance and a future in this business; I am so irresponsible and lazy; see, I told you she couldn't work; she's never going to amount to anything; she's not doing anything; she's not successful, she's a taker. Who does she think she is? You can't just up and leave a job that others would love to have? I am committed to Joy and happiness and abundance and Love. I want that more than anything. The fear of being penniless and a burden to my daughter is what keeps me stuck I think.

Thanks David for your continued dedication to healing. I await your response.

Much love.

Beloved One,

Thanks for your devotion to Awakening. As you progress inward it will be more and more evident that you are happily becoming God dependent. This is the meaning of "Except ye become as little children ye cannot enter the Kingdom of Heaven." Infants are completely dependent on their parents for survival in this world. Likewise, one must be completely dependent on the Holy Spirit to remember the Christ Self and God's Love. As you follow the Voice for God within, the doubt thoughts will continue to seem to dissolve, and your apparent "needs" as you serve the Plan will be handled miraculously. Now is a time of deepening in our shared Purpose, for this depth is required to take the steps that will surely follow.

Be gentle and kind, and nurture the Awakening of the mind by addressing whatever is placed before you. Let tomorrow take care of tomorrow. Concerns and worries about the future are never prudent or practical, for they are always based on the past.

Ease your way into Divine Providence by accepting the Peace within, and watch how effortlessly and miraculously everything is handled for you by the Holy Spirit. You are a messenger of God's Love and God's Messengers are worth their keep while they serve the Holy Spirit's Purpose. I have

an online book for you to read that will help your confidence in the Holy Spirit and Divine Providence grow in leaps and bounds: The Peace Of God Is My One Goal. (See bibliography).

Like many, you will benefit from witnesses of "being about the Holy Spirit's Purpose." You will seem to take on a lofty function as a miracle worker, for you have been Called by the Holy Spirit to this holy function. The many 'doings' on which you will be sent will bring with them much Joy. And these miracles will convince your mind that the 'laws' of the world it seemed to believe in and serve were never real. Your 'story' will be miraculous, and then you will see that you are far more than any story that ever seemed to be. You are the One!

I am joined with you in Purpose and rejoice with you as the doubt thoughts disappear from your awareness. They will all disappear. All Glory to the One Who creates Perfectly and Eternally!!!

Love, David

FORM VS. CONTENT

Dear David,

It was a rainy, foggy morning and not a particularly up day. The ACIM lesson for me today was "The Peace of God Is Shining In Me Now." As seems to be shared by many, it has been difficult for me to reconcile the Course teachings with everyday life in the world... Business worries and problems took center stage for most of the day, and at this time of the month... I mention all this to paint a portrait of my day as an example of the conflict I am experiencing.

In the late afternoon, the sun seemingly miraculously came out, and I took off on my bicycle toward the path by the river. It wasn't quite sunset and as the first formal day of fall, that moment colored the sky in perfect sync. It was suddenly so gorgeous outside.

Okay, so what's the point? It's a question, really. Given the above scenario, you'll understand if I sound a bit testy or sarcastic. If we are to believe that all of these circumstances in the world of form do not really exist, then are all the values we have associated with the pleasant and the unpleasant invalid wastes of time and energy?

Is it as pointless to allow one's self to be occasionally seduced by pleasure and beauty as it is to collapse into fear? Are they both traps? Or are these lovely experiences a glimpse of the even more splendid stuff on the other side?

I hope I am making myself clear. I think I'm feeling guilty about helping myself to feel better by seeking out the goodness in the world of form... when I am learning it is neither substantive nor meaningful. Are we to believe that the feelings we get from watching the sun set and such are merely distractions? I used to think they were gifts from God... Sometimes even signs that all is (or will be) well. Do I have to abandon that notion since it is not true? Or could it be in some way that would not compromise The Truth? Many thanks for your website and your wise counsel and gifts, and today for giving me, if nothing else, a forum in which to vent. Please attempt to enlighten when you can.

Most gratefully.

Beloved One,

Thanks for sharing and venting what is on your heart. You are dearly loved and fully appreciated. Your questions get to the subtleties of the mind training required for Awakening, because in dreaming things are not as they seem to be.

Everything that appears in this world of dreams is given its meaning by the mind of the dreamer. And the dreamer is asleep and dreaming of forms aplenty, unaware of the Abstract Light of Mind Awake. The sleeping dreamer believes in both love and fear, dissociates these feelings, projects the split onto the dream, and perceives a world of opposites as "reality." Thus beautiful and ugly, good and bad, sunny and rainy, clear and foggy, unpleasant and pleasant, etc. seem to be real descriptions of real sights and sounds and smells and conditions in the dream. There are even 'spiritual' paths that tell students to "accentuate the positive" and "eliminate the negative," as if it is possible to tell them apart.

The one right use of judgment in Awakening I call discernment. How does one feel? Is one happy, peaceful, joyful? Are one's perceptions stable and consistent? The experience one has is a barometer of the stability of one's perception. In order to be consistently peaceful, mind training is required. This involves the relinquishment of judgment; releasing the belief that one is actually capable of judging anything at all.

Each step inward is more and more humbling, until the mind reaches a point at which it can honestly say: "I do not know what anything is for." Yet this is the point at which the mind can experience the meaning of forgiveness. Be gentle with yourself on this inward journey. Accept the symbols that come to you with gladness and appreciation. Let the Holy Spirit use the symbols to remind you of the Inner Beauty that is far beyond appearances. Let the colors and the sights and smells and sounds wash through your mind as reminders of the Vastness and Glory of Being! Discover the Beauty of the Holy Spirit's Purpose.

Without judgment are all things equally acceptable. Without judgment one can see the Big Picture, the Tapestry of the Cosmos. Without judgment there is nothing 'outside' the mind and everything is therefore included.

Without judgment nothing can be rejected and there is only harmony. Without judgment, conflict and competition are no more. And without judgment One is happily, simply Being, and in this Being is everyone and everything included.

The alternative to judgment is acceptance. There is another way of looking upon the world, and this new, fresh Perspective is worth the mind training that seems to precede It. As self-concepts are laid by, so are the expectations and the stress. Behold the world anew and see a forgiven world without agendas and controls and rules. As one is light hearted, one perceives a light hearted world. Notice the synchronicities and the melody and the orchestration of the Big Picture, and observe it all with Supreme Detachment. There is a Joyful Passion in beholding all things with Detachment.

Who One is, the Christ, is truly Gorgeous. The opening to this State of Being is worthy of the attentiveness to mind training and the opening to the Holy Spirit's Purpose. True Beauty dawns as Content of Mind, and as this transformation occurs, all the forms light up and are seen as the same. It takes faith to keep attentiveness to mind training and to be open to miracles. The miracles stabilize and clear one's perception and are truly worth the effort and practice. I am joined with you in miracles and know that every bit of willingness to allow the miracle into awareness is something to rejoice about! As you proceed, the ego's emphasis on form will be eclipsed and transcended by your alignment with the Holy Spirit's Content.

In Flowing Love always, David

CALLING FORTH WITNESSES TO LOVE

Hi David.

I won't always be writing this much or this often. It will come in waves. I had an appointment with my psychiatrist today. He couldn't join us (when you visited) because he had to go out of town unexpectedly. Halfway through our visit he said, "I want you to know that your improvement is remarkable. You are much more peaceful and at ease, much more confident and seem to be very much happier. So I just want you to know that whatever interaction you had with the visiting Teacher is very obvious, very noticeable and very beneficial." I knew that, but I thought you would be interested to know that it was so vividly noticed by a psychiatrist.

Quick question: The Text keeps using the word "dissociating," what does that word mean, particularly in light of the Text's usage.

Thanks, Much Love.

Beloved One,

Thanks for this shining witness to the Power of Love. As for your question, dissociation is the attempt to forget love. It is an attempt to keep love and fear apart, for if they are brought together only love remains. This world was the attempt to believe in BOTH love and fear by dissociating them and keeping them both. Healing is bringing darkness to Light, or fear to Love, for they only seem to coexist when they have been dissociated or kept apart.

Here are some quotes from ACIM that clarify this: "Unless you first know something you cannot dissociate it. Knowledge must precede dissociation, so that dissociation is nothing more than a decision to forget. What has been forgotten then appears to be fearful, but only because the dissociation is an

attack on truth. You are fearful because you have forgotten. And you have replaced your knowledge by an awareness of dreams, because you are afraid of your dissociation, not of what you have dissociated. When what you have dissociated is accepted, it ceases to be fearful. Yet to give up the dissociation of reality brings more than merely lack of fear. In this decision lie Joy and Peace and the glory of Creation.

Offer the Holy Spirit only your willingness to remember, for He regains the knowledge of God and of yourself for you, waiting for your acceptance. Give up gladly everything that would stand in the way of your remembering, for God is in your memory. His Voice will tell you that you are part of Him when you are willing to remember Him and know your own reality again. Let nothing in this world delay your remembering of Him, for in this remembering is the knowledge of yourself. To remember is merely to restore to your mind what is already there."(T-10.II.1-2)

"Our emphasis has been on bringing what is undesirable to the desirable; what you do not want to what you do. You will realize that salvation must come to you this way, if you consider what dissociation is. Dissociation is a distorted process of thinking whereby two systems of belief which cannot coexist are both maintained. If they are brought together, their joint acceptance becomes impossible. But if one is kept in darkness from the other, their separation seems to keep them both alive and equal in their reality. Their joining thus becomes the source of fear, for if they meet, acceptance must be withdrawn from one of them. You cannot have them both, for each denies the other. Apart, this fact is lost from sight, for each in a separate place can be endowed with firm belief. Bring them together, and the fact of their complete incompatibility is instantly apparent. One will go, because the other is seen in the same place." (T-14.VII.4)

Love & Blessings, David

Pondering Thoughts on Forgiveness

David,

I have been thinking a lot lately on this issue of forgiveness. Here are my thoughts... Is it possible for me to be able to forgive? I don't think so. Not if I am thinking of it in the terms of forgetting. Yes in the terms of realizing that whatever was done, was just a mistake, and that I am going to make many more mistakes.

Is it possible for God to forgive? I again don't think so. He loves us unconditionally, which to me means he holds nothing against us. Therefore there is nothing to forgive. Where does the mistake in understanding forgiveness come from? I believe it comes from our own judgments. If I judge a person bad, or evil, dirty, or whatever in terms of what they have done (or I have perceived they have done), then it is my own personal judgments against this one. And since my judgments are personal, they must be forgiven by my own judgment rules. And these rules have nothing to do with forgiveness. They do have to do with keeping someone else under my assumed power, conditionally.

Why am I different from God, Our Father, if He is all there is. With me being an extension of Our Father, The Creator, then why do I judge, when He does not judge? This I do not know. David these are just some thoughts I have been tossing around lately.

Beloved One,

Thanks for sharing your thoughts and questions about forgiveness. Yes, God does not forgive for God has never condemned, and there must be condemnation first before forgiveness is necessary. God does Love without conditions

and Is Unconditionally Loving. God knows only Perfection, therefore God knows not of forgiveness.

The Holy Spirit, the Bridge to remembrance of God's Love, is the means of forgiveness. The Holy Spirit overlooks illusion and recognizes the Truth. The Holy Spirit's Perspective is Nonjudgmental, and by aligning with this Perspective it is apparent that it is impossible to judge. This returns awareness to Nonjudgmental Being, the Being God creates Eternally. You experience that nothing really happened at all.

The personal perspective of the ego made the world of time and space seem real. The ego was the belief in judgment, in the ability to order and rank illusions into a hierarchy. Yet given to the Holy Spirit this insane belief dissolves, for judgment never had a real source. And being without a real source judgment had no real effects. Forgiveness is seeing the impossibility of judgment and thus Awakening to the Natural State of Being Which is forever Changeless. While the belief in a future remains, forgiveness seems fearful. This is because there seems to be a "gap" of time UNTIL forgiveness is accepted. Be not content with future happiness for it is not your just reward. You have cause for freedom Now. In the Present the personal perspective is gone AND forgotten. The Kingdom of Heaven is Now!

Love always, David

AWAKENING TO CHRIST LIGHT

This message is for David…

…or whoever receives this.

First of all David has blessed my heart so very much as I had lost all sense of direction doing a comparative study of world religions. I was a fundamentalist for many years then after studying a book called *Sixteen Crucified Saviors* by Kersey Graves I was horrified to see other religions parallel with Jesus and the bible. I lost faith in Jesus for seven years but I went from one religious sect to another seeking enlightenment, talking to gurus and New Age groups. I received some pretty good tools like meditation and chanting. But my search for inner peace was in vain until I heard David a couple of Months ago over the internet.

It was God's grace I found your site and I listened in awe at what came to me was a re-conversion AWAKENING to Christ Light. I now am back to belief in Jesus and much, much more. Thank you David for being instrumental in bringing me back home to Jesus.

I have one question today. Since we are in essence in a state of perfect being and indeed always have been, then what is the need for Grace and atonement? In particular Grace? I am still very young in the Course and am sure the answer is right in front of me, but perhaps you can steer me in the right perception. Also do we who study the Course call ourselves Christian? Are you a Christian?

Beloved One,

Thanks for writing and sharing your journey, your AWAKENING to Christ Light. There are many paths in form, but the Content – Divine Love – remains Everlasting. Jesus has a way of coming back and coming back into aware-

ness, leading the seeker to the experience of the Oneness of God's Love. I am grateful to witness to the conversion from darkness to Light.

Grace is the State Of Being that knows the Truth, that One need do nothing to Be as One already Is. It is the Gift of Creation, God creating Spirit as Eternally One. Atonement is the Answer, or Correction offered to a mind asleep and dreaming of separation from God. Atonement is the one need of the sleeping mind that believes in the reality of the time-space cosmos. Atonement simply shows the false as false, for thus is the world and make-believe self forgiven. Atonement restores awareness to the ever-Present State of Grace.

You can call yourself whatever seems most Helpful at any given moment. This is a form of the Workbook Lesson: "I will step back and let Him lead the way." Let the Holy Spirit put the words in your mouth and you will always offer a blessing. When you desire to be truly Helpful, miracles occur naturally. Miracles are involuntary and should not be under conscious control. They simply flow from Love.

I am identified with God and unidentified with everything of this world. Therefore I stay aligned with the Spirit in the Now and completely unaffiliated with persons, places, things, groups, religions, countries, and concepts of time and space. Such is Happiness and Peace! I neither lead nor follow. I am. I rejoice in the Light with You Beloved of God! Light is our Home. All Glory to the One.

Love, David

DAVID AND THE MESSENGERS OF PEACE

David began his journey to spiritual enlightenment in 1986 when he encountered *A Course in Miracles* and recognized it as the tool he had been seeking for a radical transformation of his mind. He studied the Course with passionate intensity, reading it for eight or more hours a day. After two years of this study, David began attending up to five ACIM groups a week. He was startled to find that a Voice was speaking through him with great authority, so that many began referring their questions to him.

Among family members, friends and teachers, David was always known for questioning everything, rather than accepting conventional answers. Thus he was delighted to find in the Course support and encouragement from the Voice of Jesus for his careful examination of every idea, belief, concept and assumption in his mind. Jesus became David's internal teacher, answering his every question, guiding him to hand over the day-to-day management of all relationships, circumstances and events in his life, and providing inner discernment as to the writings and teachings of others. Several hermitage experiences helped David to free his mind from ego chatter and enter into deep silence, where he ultimately experienced Enlightenment.

In 1991 David was impelled to begin traveling around the United States and Canada, sharing his clarity of understanding related to *A Course in Miracles*. He followed Jesus' instructions to "become as a child", allowing himself to be totally dependent on the Holy Spirit for money, transportation, shelter, food and the words to speak in countless ACIM gatherings, churches, metaphysical and spiritual groups with everyone he met.

David found that it was his joy and peace that was the best teacher in all encounters, and that it was this peace that all his brothers and sisters were seeking. The Voice of Jesus told David – as it instructed the apostles 2,000 years before, "Freely you have received; freely give." Thus David has never charged for his time, teaching, or any of the many materials he gives away, but has been supported entirely by love offerings. In all his years of traveling and sharing the wisdom of Christ, David has become a living demonstration of the principles of *A Course In Miracles*.

In 1996 David was guided to purchase a small house in Cincinnati, Ohio, which was called the Peace House. It became a base of operations, a place of quiet and meditation between travels, and a place where he could welcome those desiring to step back from the world and go deeply within the mind to discover the Christ within. The Holy Spirit guided David to acquire computers and learn internet technology. This led to the creation of a number of websites, which today offer a huge array of resources devoted to Christ teachings, *A Course In Miracles* and metaphysics.

Since this time David has been joined by Messengers of Peace, others who have felt the Call to devote their lives fully in Service, who were inspired by David's devotion. Religious/spiritual counseling became one of the main functions of the ministry, along with travel missions and providing inspirational and deeply insightful materials. You can find the current Messengers of Peace on the Awakening Mind website.

In 1999 the non-profit Foundation for the Awakening Mind was set up as a religious education organization to support David's work.

Always a lover of music, and seeing it as a path to God in its own right, David set up a number of Music Pavilions on his website highlighting a variety of artists who share spiritual ideas through music. Also available on the site are video clips of television interviews and gatherings, audio recordings of gatherings and teaching sessions, searchable archives, and many deep writings. David discovered movies as another helpful path to God, and *The Movie Watcher's Guide To Enlightenment* was Given by the Spirit as another wonderful Awakening resource.

In 2003 with an invitation to Argentina, the international travels beyond Canada began, and since then David has traveled to 22 countries, shining the Light and sharing the message of Truth.

From 2005 onward, friends around the world began opening their homes as Peace Houses with a strong desire to abide by the Guidelines of the Peace House in Cincinnati and remain in close contact with David and the Messengers. These Peace Houses make Awakening Mind materials available to the public, host gatherings/retreats and are quiet bases during travels.

During 2006 and 2007 the Messengers of Peace joined with inspired volunteers in a worldwide collaborative venture to launch the Teacher of Teachers website, a site hosting the most advanced teachings of *A Course In Miracles*, set in the form of an Awakening curriculum. This website will continue to be added to as a vast vault of materials is converted to MP3 format and transcribed by volunteers. The Awakening Mind website was translated into Spanish and French. The Foundation began using MissionFish, an online nonprofit organization set up with eBay Giving Works to make materials available.

In 2007 the Awakening Mind International Retreat Center was purchased by the Foundation, and throughout 2008 it has been used to host visitors from around the world for weekend retreats and Devotional stays. This year David also fulfilled a project dear to his heart, the emergence of a low-cost Spanish edition of ACIM for South American countries.

In 2008 the Teacher of Teachers website was translated into Portuguese. Awakening Mind Europe, an online communications & networking site, was launched along with other technological advances in communications. Houses near to the Peace House in Cincinnati are being rented to accommodate devoted volunteers. And, *Healing In Mind* was published!

David and the Messengers of Peace continue to travel where invited to share practical gatherings that inspire and bless all who come seeking peace of mind.

Coming together with the Messengers of Peace is a chance to join with the shared intention of uncovering the beliefs that seem to obstruct the awareness of Love's presence. Gatherings and retreats are opportunities for bringing concerns and questions to the surface of awareness, seeking for clarity from those who rely entirely on the Spirit to answer from a perspective that is beyond the personal. The result of learning the Holy Spirit's purpose of forgiveness leads to the peace, happiness and freedom that is Reality.

Awakening to Who You Are has no price or cost. Love offerings, gifts and donations are gratefully accepted to support the Foundation and its works.

We welcome all inquiries and requests from anyone with a deep, sincere desire to Awaken to Eternal Love. Always feel free to send a letter or an e-mail and feel free to call and speak with one of us.

BIBLIOGRAPHY

A Course in Miracles, second. ed.
Foundation for Inner Peace.
Mill Valley , CA 1996

Music of Christ, Resta:
http://awakening-mind.org/moc-download.htm

Psychotherapy: Purpose, Process, and Practice,
Foundation for Inner Peace.
Tiburon, CA 1978

Purpose is the only Choice:
Hoffmeister, David,
http://awakening-mind.org/library/bookspubs/purpose.html

The Urantia Book, part IV, The Life of Jesus,
New York: Uversa Press, 2003

Main Awakening Mind Sites

http://awakening-mind.org
http://miracleshome.org

Awakening In Christ Yahoo Group
Global Mailing List

http://groups.yahoo.com/group/awakeninginchrist

ADDITIONAL
AWAKENING MIND RESOURCES

Video

http://acim-online-video.net/
http://jesus-christ-videos.net/
http://video.yahoo.com/search?ytag=1&p=david+hoffmeister
http://video.google.com/videosearch?q=david+hoffmeister

Audio

http://awakening-mind.org/mp3gatherings.htm
http://a-course-in-miracles.org http://miracleshome.org/
MP3/europe2008.htm
http://miracleshome.org/MP3/easter2007.htm
http://miracles-org.us

eBay
http://course-in-miracles.us

Contact Us

requests@awakening-mind.org
retreats@awakening-mind.org

To order Healing In Mind

http://davidhoffmeistermaterials.com
(Independent commercial website that supports the
Foundation for the Awakening Mind)

You need be neither careful nor careless;
you need merely cast your cares upon Him
because He careth for you.

(T-5.VII.1)